LET'S W

Series E

Central England

Robert Kirk

Line drawings by the author

JAVELIN BOOKS

POOLE · NEW YORK · SYDNEY

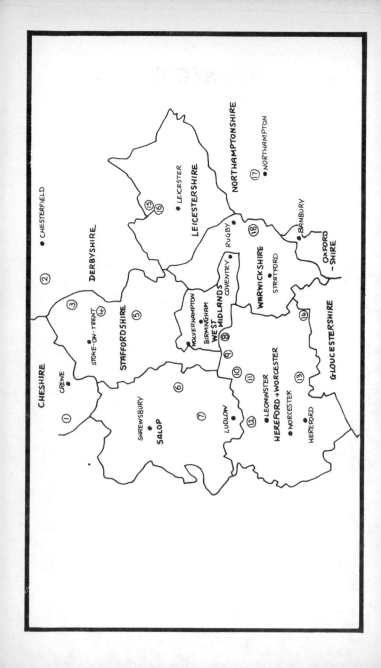

CONTENTS

First published in the UK 1987 by Javelin Books,
Link House, West Street, Poole, Dorset, BH15 1LL

Copyright © 1987 Javelin Books

Distributed in Australia by
Capricorn Link (Australia) Pty Ltd,
PO Box 665, Lane Cove, NSW 2066

British Library Cataloguing in Publication Data

Kirk, Robert, *1932-*
    Central England. —(Let's walk there!)
    1. Midlands (England) —Description and
    travel—Guide-books
    I. Title   II. Series
    914.24'04858   DA670.M64
        ISBN 0 7137 1769 6

Cover picture:
Shugborough Hall courtesy of The British Tourist
Authority, Britain on View (BTA/ETB)

Cartography by Ron Rigby

Typeset by Inforum Ltd, Portsmouth
Printed in Great Britain by Cox & Wyman Ltd, Reading, Berks.

INTRODUCTION

As worthwhile as any walk might be, it becomes doubly appealing if it takes you to some place of special interest. The nine books in this series, covering England, Scotland and Wales were conceived to describe just such walks.

A full description of the walk's objective is given at the start of each chapter. The objectives are diverse, giving a wide choice. Most are non-seasonal, and involve little walking in themselves once you are there.

Following the description of the objective, each section of the walk is clearly described, and a specially drawn map makes route-finding straightforward. As well as detailing the route, the authors describe many subsidiary points of interest encountered along the way.

The walks are varied and easy to follow. None of them is too taxing, except in the severest weather. Most are circular, returning you to your car at the starting point. Family walkers with young children will find plenty of shorter routes to suit their particular needs, whilst those with longer legs can select from more substantial walks.

The routes have been carefully chosen to include only well-established routes, and readers will certainly increase the enjoyment which they and others derive from the country-side if they respect it by following the Country Code.

Bruce Bedford
Series Editor

ACKNOWLEDGEMENTS

Walks 15, 16, 17, and 18 I did in the company of Fred Clapham of the Rugby Group of the Ramblers' Association and I must thank him for suggesting them. Credit for including the best bits of these walks is claimed by each of us; any mistakes are the fault of the other.

Robert Kirk

Walk 1
RAWHEAD
CHESHIRE
8 miles

Rawhead is the highest point of the Sandstone Trail, a long-distance path stretching 30 miles from Overon Hill, Frodsham, to Grindley Brook on the Shropshire county boundary.

The sandstone scarp at Rawhead reaches 746 feet and makes a superb viewpoint across a patchwork of fields bounded by oak-dotted hedgerows to the mountains of Wales.

Earth movements have led to fracturing and tilting of the blocks of rock, pushing up ridges to a height where they escaped being covered with clay, sand, and gravel carried by the last Ice Age glaciers.

There are several caves, once excavated for fine sand to scour cottage floors, some with names derived from local folklore which has given rise to many stories associated with them.

Start from an old sand quarry near the Sandstone Trail at Duckington. The quarry makes a pleasant secluded car park. To reach the narrow lane leading to the quarry from the A41(T) north of Whitchurch, *either:* (1) Turn onto an unclassified road at the island of Hampton Heath. Turn left at Ashton Cross and the lane is on the right after one and a half miles *or*, (2) Turn onto the A534 at the island at Broxton. In three quarters of a mile take the unclassified road sign-posted to Duckington. The lane is on the left after one and three-quarter miles.

RAWHEAD

1 mile

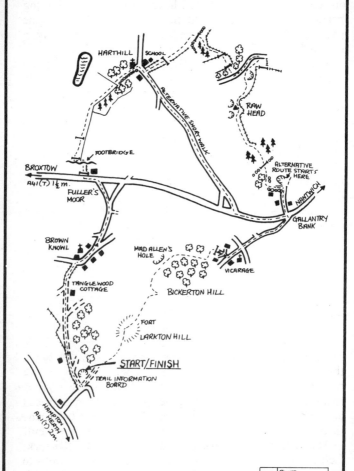

HARTHILL
SCHOOL
ALTERNATIVE SHORT WALK
RAW HEAD
ALTERNATIVE ROUTE STARTS HERE
FOOTBRIDGE
BROXTOW
A41 (T) 1½ m.
FULLER'S MOOR
NANTWICH
GALLANTRY BANK
BROWN KNOWL
MAD ALLEN'S HOLE
VICARAGE
TANGLEWOOD COTTAGE
BICKERTON HILL
FORT
LARKTON HILL
START/FINISH
TRAIL INFORMATION BOARD
HAMPTON HEATH
A41 (T) 2m.

	ROUTE
	ROAD
	GATE OR STILE
	FENCE
	STONE WALL
	SLOPE

The first stage of the walk leads from the quarry entrance to the small village of Brown Knowl. Follow the wide sandy lane northwards to a log barrier. Take the left-hand track at the barrier; it climbs gradually for quarter of a mile and levels out on an open birch-covered heath. Descend left to a log barrier and continue straight ahead on the unsurfaced lane past Tanglewood Cottage. The lane ends on a tarmac road in the village.

Turn right through the village passing the gates of the Methodist Church. Keep left, then right, then left at the next three road junctions (ignore the farm track to the right) to reach the A453 at Fuller's Moor. Follow to the left until opposite a farmhouse where a stile and footpath sign mark a path leading northwards. Follow the field edge to a footbridge. Cross into the next field and turn left to a waymarked stile on the corner. Cross, and follow the hedge uphill to the next stile. The path continues uphill along the wire fence to the Pine Tree Plantation on top of the hill.

Continue along the headland close to the wood. A coppice replaces the pines and a gate gives access to a green lane.

The green lane ends at the church of All Saints, Harthill. The tiny sandstone church's open belfry is crowned by a short spire supported on four columns. A cluster of stone houses and the village school fringe a kind of green. Turn right in front of the school to where a footpath sign points down a green lane and follow this to its end.

Cross the stile at the lane end and follow the hedge uphill to a pine-covered sandstone knoll. Follow the wall bordering the wood until a ladder stile allows you to cross. Go uphill through the wood and maintain height above the conifers to a wooden squeezer stile in a wire fence. Descend across a field to a waymarked stile in the hedge bordering an unsurfaced lane. Continue uphill through the wood to a surfaced lane then uphill along the lane to where the angle eases at a bend.

At the bend a footpath sign points uphill; follow to a fork. Left leads steeply uphill for adventurous souls. It climbs to where rocks force a deviation left to a wire fence. Follow this uphill to where it strikes the crest at a stile on the Sandstone

Robert Kirk

A line of rocky outcrops on the Sandstone Trail at Rawhead makes a series of attractive vantage points

Trail. The original path through the woodland takes a more gentle ascent but offers the mild excitement of a traverse along the narrow ledges of a low sandstone crag at the top. This path strikes the crest of the ridge at a waymark post 200 yards north of the triangulation point on Rawhead.

The walk now follows the clearly waymarked Sandstone Trail over Rawhead and on to Larkton Hill. At Rawhead itself the ground drops steeply away to the top of vertical sandstone crags. Along the length of the ridge are uninterrupted views across the Cheshire Plain. Westwards lie the mountains of Wales and northwards the distinctive shapes of Helsby Hill and Overton Hill mark the south bank of the Mersey Estuary.

The trail follows a twisting course along the crest of the escarpment and finally descends through birches to a footpath sign in a broken wall. From here an unsurfaced lane leads to an old quarry. A signpost points the way and the lane ends on the A534 at Gallantry Bank. Opposite, a trail signpost points down the lane to Bickerton. Continue over the crossroads at Bickerton Church to the Vicarage where a trail signpost points right to Larkton Hill.

A stile is crossed and then the path climbs gently uphill over sandy heath with birch and bilberry. At Bickerton Hill the path strikes the crest of the ridge at another fine viewpoint above Mad Allen's Hole. Waymarks and a welltrodden track indicate the route to Larkton Hill where there are the remains of a hill fort. The meandering course of the Dee can be traced on the plain below, particularly when the water reflects the afternoon sun. Beyond the river is Ruabon Mountain west of Wrexham and the now familiar skyline of the Berwyns. On the southern horizon are the Briedden Hills near Welshpool and slightly east of them, and nearer, the wooded tops of Grinshill and Hawkstone Park.

From Larkton Hill the trail descends to a waymark which points to the information board near the quarry at the start of the walk.

Walk 2
HADDON HALL
DERBYSHIRE
$3\frac{3}{4}$ miles

The stone battlements on the walls and towers of Haddon Hall, and the plan arranged around two courtyards separated by the Great Hall have their origins in medieval fortification. Haddon, though, was never built to withstand a siege. Extensions and improvements were made by successive generations of Vernons and Manners from the twelfth to the seventeenth centuries, and features of the architectural styles of these years still remain.

In 1703, when the Manners became the Dukes of Rutland, they abandoned Haddon in favour of Belvoir Castle. Haddon thereby escaped the classical restructuring favoured by eighteenth century fashion. It remains today as an authentic example of the building styles of Tudor and Elizabethan England.

Opening times are from March to October, 11am to 6pm; closed Mondays, except Bank Holidays, and on Sundays during July and August.

Start from the National Park Information Centre in Bridge Street near the centre of Bakewell. There are car parks behind the Information Centre and near the river. The centre stands in the town's old Market Hall which, although recently restored, dates back to the sixteenth century.

Walk along Bridge Street and take the riverside walk starting at the Bridge House Restaurant. The path is a convenient place from which to look back at Bakewell Bridge which carries the main road northwards out of the town over

12

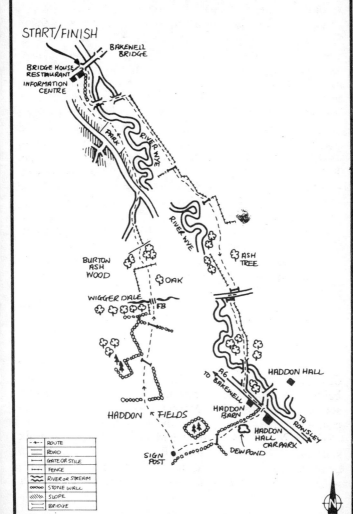

HADDON HALL

1 mile

START/FINISH

BAKEWELL BRIDGE

BRIDGE HOUSE RESTAURANT

INFORMATION CENTRE

PARK

RIVER WYE

RIVER WYE

ASH TREE

BURTON ASH WOOD

OAK

WIGGER DALE

FB

HADDON HALL

A.6 TO BAKEWELL

HADDON BARN

HADDON HALL CAR PARK

TO ROWSLEY

HADDON FIELDS

DEW POND

SIGN POST

	ROUTE
	ROAD
	GATE OR STILE
	FENCE
	RIVER OR STREAM
	STONE WALL
	SLOPE
	BRIDGE

N

the River Wye. There has been a bridge here since Saxon times and the present one preserves the stone pointed-arch construction of the thirteenth century.

A footbridge takes our path across the Wye and shortly a second footbridge gives access to the agricultural show-ground. A wide surfaced road runs from the showground office to a gate and stile in the southern boundary fence. From here the scenery of the valley attracts more interest. The path continues along the line of a hedge to a plank footbridge. The Wye, meandering gently on its flood plane, swings close to the path at this point. The river is fringed with alder and the next half a mile will hold particularly the interest of birdwatchers at all seasons of the year.

Beyond the footbridge a low waymarked post points left to a stile in a wooden fence which marks the boundary of a coppice on the riverbank. This choice of path keeps above the level of the river and is a drier alternative to the path through the coppice at the waterline. The southern end of the lower path is signposted for the benefit of walkers coming in that direction.

The route now approaches a stile near a large mature oak. Do not cross the stile but take the direction indicated by a waymark arrow. This leads across the pasture to an ash tree with a split trunk and then to a wicket gate leading to an unsurfaced lane.

At the lane turn right towards the river for 20 yards. The path is here signposted to Haddon Hall ½ mile at a stile in a metal rail fence. The path squeezes between a fence and a bend in the river; an obstacle course of wooden planks is some help over the wetter parts. Haddon Hall can now be seen through the trees. The path, still liable to be muddy underfoot, is now confined between wire fences leading to a concrete footbridge over the Wye. Beyond the bridge the path rises to a squeezer stile in a stone wall. You are now on the A6 roughly 200 yards from the entrance to Haddon Hall.

The start of the continuation of the walk is signposted at a gate in the field adjacent to Haddon Hall visitor's car park. Cross the field to a second gate. Ignore the signpost pointing

Haddon Hall stands close to the River Derwent in a peaceful parkland setting

to Alport and follow the unsurfaced track keeping to the line of the stone wall. This rises gently, passing a walled dew-pond, to a metal field gate. The track continues now with the wall on the left and gradually gains height into the open pasture of Haddon Fields.

This is a good vantage point at which to pause and look back across the valley to Haddon Hall. It is a beautiful setting, and the quality of the scenery owes much to the foresight of the 5th Duke of Rutland who established the woodlands in the park of Haddon Hall.

The next objective is a signpost placed at a squeezer in the wall. It marks the direction to Wigger Dale, three quarters of a mile, and hence to Bakewell. The route is straightforward, beginning with level walking across Haddon Fields in the direction indicated by the signpost. On this stretch there are good views across the valley to the gritstone moorlands north of Baslow.

The path crosses a stone wall at a squeezer and then runs across the next field to a wooden stile in a broken wall. From here, descend gradually to another stile and then more steeply down into Wigger Dale. The stream in the dale is crossed by a plank bridge at the corner of a wood. It then crosses the brow of the next field to a stile in a wooden fence bordering Burton Ashes Wood.

The path through the wood is clear of undergrowth and leads easily to the stile at the exit. It is placed near a fine beech and has circular concrete footsteps. A low hawthorn hedge marks the line of what was once a sunken lane which now leads through an old orchard to an unsurfaced lane leading steeply down to the A6 at the outskirts of Bakewell.

A path which makes a better alternative than the main road starts on the opposite side of the A6 a few yards in the direction of Bakewell. A squeezer stile in the wall marks the beginning of a footpath which crosses allotments near the river and on between adjoining back gardens. It finally leads out into the park in Haddon Road and the Information Centre is reached in less than half a mile.

Walk 3
THOR'S CAVE
STAFFORDSHIRE
5 miles

The limestone dales of the Peak District are famous for their crags and pinnacles which have weathered into spectacular shapes. There are few crags in the southern Peak which offer the ordinary walker such a dramatic and commanding viewpoint as the one containing Thor's Cave in the Manifold valley. The crag rises out of a steep wooded hillside high above the valley floor, the cave at its base commanding a fine view northwards along the meandering course of the river.

5,000 years ago Stone Age men migrated into the Peak and made their home in Thor's and similar caves in the locality. The floor of Thor's Cave has yielded a variety of animal bones and evidence of cooking activities. It is probable that the cave was used by men for thousands of years, the way of life of the inhabitants changing from that of the itinerant hunter to the settled cave dweller of pre-Roman times.

This walk starts from the village of Wetton in the White Peak. Take the minor road to Alstonefield which leaves the A515 Ashbourne to Buxton road opposite the New Inns Hotel five and a half miles north of Ashbourne. The twisting lanes leading to Wetton are clearly signed from Alstonefield. There is a car park on a lane leading off the south end of the main street; the walk begins from here.

Turn right out of the car park and then right again at the T-junction. Leave the village on the lane leading to Wetton Mill; in a few yards a narrow walled lane leads off to the left. This is signposted as a concessionary path to Thor's Cave.

THOR'S CAVE

1 mile

- BROAD ECTON FARM
- CANTRELL'S HOUSE
- LEE'S FARM
- SUGAR LOAF
- DALE FARM
- CAVES
- WETTON MILL
- WETTON HILL
- MANOR HOUSE FARM
- TO BUTTERTON
- TO WETTON
- TO WETTON MILL
- TO HARTINGTON
- WETTON
- TO ILAM
- START/FINISH
- RIVER MANIFOLD
- THOR'S CAVE

		ROUTE
		ROAD
		GATE or STILE
		FENCE
		RIVER or STREAM
		STONE WALL
		BRIDGE

N

The grassy lane offers easy walking and the vertical crag which has Thor's Cave at its base is already a prominent feature of the view ahead. The path leaves the lane after half a mile just beyond a field gate. A stile in the right-hand wall gives access to the adjoining field. Cross the stile and walk downhill, aiming for a stile set in a wire fence near a tree. Beyond the fence a narrow path crosses steep ground to the base of the crag.

The cave at close quarters is impressive; the scramble up into the entrance is not difficult and the interior is worth exploring. The mouth of the cave frames an impressive view of the Manifold valley.

A stepped path has been constructed from just below the cave entrance to combat erosion on the well-used descent into the Manifold valley. Descending such paths can be jarring and tedious and the steps can be avoided half-way down the descent by taking a path which crosses a stile in a wire fence to the right.

This public path joins a path which has followed a little side valley leading down to the Manifold from Wetton. A wooden signpost marks the junction and from here the gradients down to the footbridge over the river are easy.

Cross the footbridge and follow the surfaced walkway which runs along the valley to Wetton Mill. It follows the former track of the Leek and Manifold Light Railway, opened in 1904, whose chief use was to carry milk from the valley farms. It linked with the railway at Waterhouses and became a tourist attraction before it finally closed in 1934.

The old line winds through a half-mile of delightful limestone valley and crosses the river to meet the road from Wetton to Butterton. Directly across the road the walkway continues along the valley to Wetton Mill. The walk crosses the river to the mill by the wide packhorse bridge built by the Duke of Devonshire in 1807. Packhorses were used to carry copper ore from the mines at Ecton further up the valley.

Wetton Mill, now owned by the National Trust and providing refreshments, ceased as a corn mill in 1857. It is attractively set below a small limestone outcrop.

The entrance to Thor's Cave frames an impressive view across the Manifold Valley

Continue on the road to Dale Farm and the start of a footpath to Back of Ecton. The path goes through a gate on the left of the farmhouse and on through a metal field gate up a dry valley.

Sugar Loaf, a steep little hill with limestone outcrops on its slopes, blocks the end of the valley. Avoid the top by climbing steeply up to the left, then cross flatter ground to a squeezer in a dry wall. Go through and immediately cross the fence on the left by a wooden rail stile. Follow the fence northwards and pass through a gap between the fence and a wall.

At a right-angle bend in the fence a low stone wall runs northwards and the right of way follows the right-hand side of it. There are two gaps and a gate to negotiate and then the path meets the drive of Broad Ecton Farm.

Turn right along the drive which climbs over a rise. The unsurfaced drive descends to a stand of trees at the entrance gate of Lees Farm. Leave the drive near the gate and descend to two stiles in broken dry-stone walls bordering an old cart track. The second stile gives access to a large field and the path runs diagonally across it to a stile in the far boundary fence.

Cross the stile and the path leads out onto the wide open grassy slopes of Wetton Hill. The path follows an easterly line keeping near a wire fence and section of wall. Find a dry firm course on grass round the northern side of the hill. The gradient eventually eases and a length of dry-stone wall projects across the line of the path. Go through the wide gap in the wall and continue round the base of the hill to the next wall.

Keep the wall on your left for the length of two fields. A squeezer allows access into the third field which has two squeezers in its southern boundary wall: go through the right-hand, higher, one. From here it should be easy to trace the line of the path across a succession of narrow fields by sighting the squeezer in the next wall. The path finally ends at a gate near the outbuildings of Manor House Farm in Wetton.

Walk 4
ALTON
STAFFORDSHIRE
6 or 3¾ miles

Alton is a lovely village in a secluded stretch of the Churnet valley in north Staffordshire. A castle was built at Alton around 1175, by Bertram of Verdun, a faithful follower of Henry II, on an imposing sandstone rock which overlooks the valley. Bertram's castle has been replaced by a romantic mirage of Rhineland designed by the Victorian architect A.W.N. Pugin, giving expression to a romantic ideal cherished by the 16th Earl of Shrewsbury. The earl wanted to create a self-contained religious community where the poor of the parish would receive education and shelter. Around a quadrangle on the old castle site Pugin designed a church, a school, a hospice for the old and almshouses for the poor. The last two are now a convent and the castle is a boarding school.

The village of Oakamoor lies on the B5417 three miles east of Cheadle. Staffordshire County Council have landscaped a picnic site with a car park in the centre of the village which can be used to start the longer walk.

The narrow road which passes the entrance to the picnic site winds along the Churnet valley to Alton. An alternative start to the walk can be made at Lord's Bridge, mid-way between Oakamoor and Alton. There is parking space near the Ramblers' Retreat, a brick-built Victorian lodge which is now a coffee house and restaurant.

Leave the picnic site by crossing the river and follow the old siding which links with the former railway at the ruins of Oakamoor Station. The old line makes a pleasant walk along

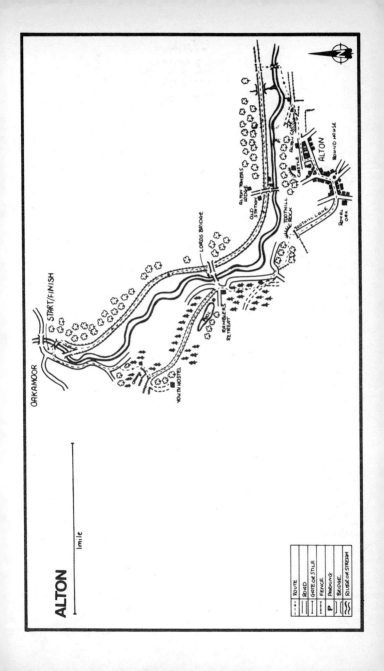

the valley floor. In one and a half miles the line passes below a sandstone outcrop and on under a bridge.

(Walkers using the alternative start join the line here. A path starts from the Ramblers' Retreat and crosses Lord's Bridge, a stone arched bridge over the Churnet. Almost immediately the incline on the north side of the railway bridge gives access to the old line.)

The turrets of Alton Castle soon appear high above the wooded slopes of the valley. In half a mile the walkway reaches the grand lodge-like structure of Alton Station. Continue under the bridge. The valley has a more open aspect as the ground on the south side of the valley becomes less steep. In half a mile the walkway crosses a viaduct and roughly 100 yards beyond it is a broken kissing gate on the right of the track.

Go through and cross the footbridge over the river. Uphill is a farm with a prominent brick barn. The path crosses the field between the barn and the river to a wooden squeezer stile in the corner bordering the farm drive.

Cross the drive and follow a wide grassy promenade contouring the side of the valley. Do not be lured too far along its easy gradient but look instead for a path which climbs steeply towards the base of Alton Cliff. This leads to a nice situation with a line of sandstone outcrops overhanging woodland which has fine chestnut and oak trees. Below, the Churnet flows through flat watermeadows.

The path finds a break in the line of crags and crosses more level ground then another wooden squeezer in a wire fence. To the right now can be seen the farm buildings at Town Head on the outskirts of Alton village. Cross the field towards the buildings; a pair of cattlegrids with waymarked stiles alongside lead to the road.

Follow the road into the village. At the entrance drive of the castle turn left passing the parish church and right along High Street with the oldest buildings in the village. The White Hart is the most ancient; the site on which it is based once stood inside the curtain wall of the Norman castle.

Leave High Street along Smithy Bank at the top of which is

Alton Castle stands on a commanding site in the Churnet Valley once occupied by a medieval fortress

the Round House or lock-up. It is a listed building built in 1830 to imprison drunks and felons awaiting trial. Keep right at the Round House and walk down Knight Lane to the Royal Oak.

At the right of the Royal Oak a bridleway post marks the start to Toothill Lane. From here to the Ramblers' Retreat the walk follows the Staffordshire Way, waymarked by posts bearing the Staffordshire Knot symbol. Toothill Lane is a wide stony track which ends at a gate near Toothill Rock, a fine viewpoint.

The path maintains height, keeping near the upper edge of Toothill Wood, and passes below a small sandstone outcrop overhung with beech trees. At the end of the outcrop, descend steeply alongside a wire fence to the Alton–Oakamoor road.

Leave the road at the bend along an unsurfaced track signposted 'Smelting Mill ½m, Dimmingsdale ¾m'. The walk is aiming for the first of these destinations. The track has been cut through a band of sandstone and tops a gentle rise. Pines and rhododendrons flank the way here; be careful not to miss a narrow path which descends on the right to the Ramblers' Retreat.

The continuation of the walk to Oakamoor also follows part of the Staffordshire Way. A wide sandy path heads up Ousal Dale from the Ramblers' Retreat passing the pool behind the old smelting mill. Beyond the pool the path ascends through plantations of young larch to a Staffordshire Way finger post placed at the head of the dale.

Leave the Staffs Way at the finger post and go through the gate in the wall on the right. Follow the walled lane towards a cottage. Just before the cottage a squeezer in the left-hand wall gives access to the conifer plantation on Moss Banks. The descent through the plantation is steep at first, then the conifers give way to mixed deciduous woodland of oak, chestnut and beech. The path finally joins the road at the end of a high stone retaining wall just under half a mile from the picnic site in Oakamoor.

Walk 5
SHUGBOROUGH HALL
STAFFORDSHIRE
6 or 5½ miles

Shugborough Hall, on the northern edge of Cannock Chase in Staffordshire, is the home of the fifth Earl of Lichfield, better known as the royal photographer Patrick Lichfield. The hall was renovated in Regency Style between 1790 and 1806 by Samuel Wyatt. Wyatt was also responsible for the portico in which each column is made of wood faced with slate, an unusual practice.

The hall is now the property of the National Trust and is managed by Staffordshire County Council. The old stable block and kitchen wing now houses the county museum. There is also a farm museum which preserves rare local breeds of farm livestock, such as Bagot goats and Tamworth pigs. The hall is open to the public from March 15 to October 26: Tuesday–Friday (including Good Friday and Bank Holiday Monday) 10.30am–5.30pm; Weekends, 2pm–5.30pm.

At the entrance to Shugborough's park is the Essex Bridge, a superb seventeenth-century packhorse bridge spanning the River Trent. It derives its name from the Earl of Essex who commissioned it. It is reputed to have had 40 arches originally, but today there are only 14. Nevertheless, it is an impressive and attractive structure and is claimed to be the longest packhorse bridge in England.

Cannock Chase was designated an Area of Outstanding Natural Beauty in 1958 and it has become deservedly popular with Midlands town dwellers as a place of escape on summer weekends. This walk crosses the northern end of the Chase

SHUGBOROUGH HALL

1 mile

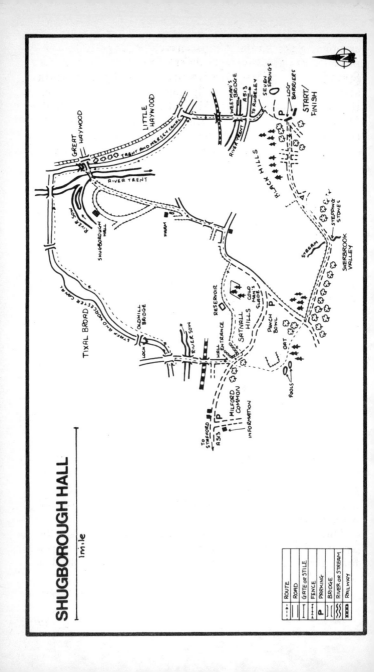

- - - -	ROUTE
‖	ROAD
⊢⊣	GATE or STILE
┬┬┬	FENCE
P	PARKING
═══	BRIDGE
≋	RIVER or STREAM
▦	RAILWAY

GREAT HAYWOOD

LITTLE HAYWOOD

TRENT AND MERSEY CANAL

WESTMAN'S BRIDGE

A513

To RUGELEY

SEVEN SPRINGS

LOW BARRIERS

P

START/FINISH

RIVER TRENT

RIVER TRENT

BLACK HILLS

STEPPING STONES

SHERBROOK VALLEY

STREAM

RIVER SOW

SHUGBOROUGH HALL

FARM

TIXALL BROAD

STAFF AND WORCESTER CANAL

OLD HILL BRIDGE

LOCK

RIVER SOW

RESERVOIR

HALL ENTRANCE

SATNALL HILLS

COLD MAN'S SLADE

P

PUNCH BOWL

OAT

POOLS

To STAFFORD A513

A513

P

MILFORD COMMON

INFORMATION

and then seeks out quiet but scenic canal towpaths to complete its circuit. The route description starts from Seven Springs car park. Space here is restricted and if your visit is in summer and you find Seven Springs too congested, alternative starting points are at Milford Common, Cold Man's Slade, and the Punch Bowl. All of these car parks are easily accessible from the A513 Stafford to Rugeley road.

At Seven Springs log barriers are placed across the paths leading from the car park. Take the wide stony track leading from the right-hand barrier; where it forks, at an emergency access notice, keep right. The track holds a fairly level course through bracken and scattered groups of trees, maintaining some distance from the conifer plantations covering the Black Hills.

After three quarters of a mile the path follows the wire fence bordering a conifer plantation. Old oaks, remnants of the ancient natural forest, have been preserved at the edge of the plantation. The path finally descends into Sherbrook Valley at some stepping stones. In many ways this is the most pleasant valley on Cannock Chase. It is graced with tall birches, and some alder in the wetter places.

Cross the stepping stones and turn right towards Milford. There is no mistaking the way: a wide stony track leads below pleasant mixed woodland cover on the rising ground to the left. In half a mile the track turns sharp right to join the A513 at the Punch Bowl car park.

The walk leaves the track at this bend; there is a post which indicates the direction to Milford. This path needs a bit of effort for it climbs steeply upwards through birch woodland to Oat Hill. Other tracks converge from all sides as the ground levels out near the top. Keep on the widest path until a diversion can be made leftwards to a group of three old Scots pines on the top of the hill.

This is a good viewpoint from which to gaze out across the Trent valley. Neighbouring Spring Hill is also topped by a few pines, and the unmistakable shape of Stafford Castle is seen in the far distance.

Rejoin the wide path used on the way up and continue

Robert Kirk

Parkland with newly planted trees complements the elegant facade of Shugborough Hall

towards Milford. It begins to descend to a small pool and passes between two bracken-covered knolls to where a second pool comes into view. Directly ahead the ground falls away to Milford Common but the walk keeps to a path which maintains height and leads to a small stand of conifers. From here it descends to the A513 opposite an entrance to Shugborough park.

A longer diversion begins at the park entrance, following the lane towards Tixall and joining the towpath of the Staffs and Worcester Canal. The canal is interesting. It is widened at Tixall Road because James Brindley, who supervised its construction, was asked to make the canal look like a natural lake when it came within sight of Tixall Hall. Tixall Broad remains as a haven for wildlife but Tixall Hall has now been demolished. The diversion ends when the towpath of the Trent and Mersey Canal is joined near Great Haywood.

The shorter walk goes alongside the park wall on the A513 and then crosses Satnall Hills to Cold Man's Slade car park. At the end of the wall the path climbs uphill alongside a fence to the hall reservoir. There are alternative routes down but the most direct starts as a grassy path through birches and descends to the left of a plantation directly to the car park.

Continue on the A513 towards Rugeley to a signpost marking the start of a bridleway to Great Haywood. The bridleway follows a surfaced estate road through the park, and the entrance to the farm as well as the entrance to the hall lead off it.

The bridleway leaves the park and crosses Essex Bridge. Immediately, the lane rises to the hump-backed bridge over the Trent and Mersey Canal. The towpath is reached through a gap in the wall on the right of the lane. The towpath offers a pleasant mile of easy walking, and the views from the towpath across the water meadows of the meandering Trent to the hills of Cannock Chase are satisfying.

The towpath is left at Bridge 72 near Little Haywood. Join the lane which goes under the main Trent Valley railway line and over the Trent on Weetman's Bridge. The lane joins the A513 opposite the entrance to the Seven Springs car park.

Walk 6
BENTHALL HALL
SHROPSHIRE
6¼ miles

The Ironbridge Gorge Museum sites attract many visitors, but few who cross Abraham Darby's cast iron bridge go on to explore the footpaths on Benthall Edge leading to Benthall Hall.

Benthall Hall is Tudor, but its exact date is uncertain – probably around 1583. The Benthalls were Catholics and the house was garrisoned in 1642 during the Civil War, but most of the panelling, richly carved staircase and Jacobean ceilings have survived.

The house, now in the care of the National Trust, is open from Easter Sunday to 30 September, 2pm to 6pm on Tuesdays, Wednesdays, and Saturdays.

Start at the car park on the south bank of the Severn at the Iron Bridge. Follow the railway walk to the Bower Yard Picnic Site where boats were made when the Severn was used as a navigation. At the entrance to the site is a map of the Benthall Edge Nature Trail, sections of which are used on this walk.

Cross the bridge over the old railway to Post 1 of the trail. The bridge and the post mark the line of an inclined plane which was used to transport clay from pits on the hillside to a brickworks on the river bank. Walk the short stage to Post 2, next to which is an old adit or drift mine. Continue along the path until it descends to a point where the railway walk can be joined. By an information notice about coppicing management, take to the path which rises fairly steeply uphill,

BENTHALL HALL

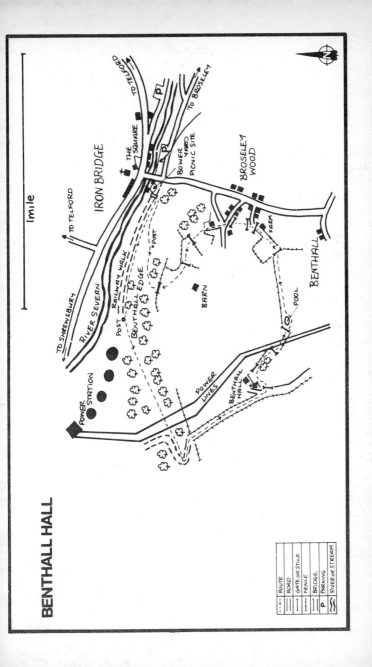

marked by a line of wooden fencing posts. The effort expended in taking the higher path is repaid by better views across the gorge. The Severn Warehouse, one of the Gorge Museum's sites lies across the river and the prominent limestone scar on the hillside across the gorge marks the site of the collapsed limestone caverns on Lincoln Hill.

The walk is now back on a section of the nature trail. The cooling towers of the electricity generating station are an unavoidable intrusion for the next half a mile or so. At Post 16 the walk leaves the nature trail again. A public footpath continues up the valley at a fairly gentle gradient for a mile through pleasant woodland. Parts of the woodland were removed by industrial activity and the disturbed areas have been recolonised by sycamore. Current management of the woods is designed to remove this species and to encourage the regeneration of ash and elm.

Soon the sounds of the power station in the narrow confines of the gorge fade, and the view opens across the valley to Buildwas. The woodland path joins a stony track: go to the left, round a U-bend and on to a metal field gate. Beyond, an unsurfaced lane leads out of the woodland across fields to Benthall Hall and church.

The walk between Benthall Hall and Ironbridge runs along clearly waymarked footpaths; all of this work was done voluntarily by members of the Broseley and Wenlock Group of the Ramblers' Association. Walk from the entrance gate of the Hall to the end of the churchyard wall. At the side of the lane there is an unusual stile with cantilevered rails weighted at one end; press the top rail and step over. The path continues across the field in front of the Hall to a stile and gate in a wire fence. Do not cross this stile but turn right and follow the fence and avenue of trees for 400 yards to a gate and stile. Cross into the next field and continue in the same direction alongside the fence to another waymarked stile. Continue in the direction of the waymark arrow past a pool to the next stile. Again an arrow points the way; follow the hedge to a gate leading into a grassy lane ending at a farm.

Keep out of the farm yard by using the stile on the left of

BENTHALL CHURCH
AND HALL

Robert Kirk

Benthall Hall and Church stand isolated in open country on the edge of the Severn Gorge

the lane. Keep close to the barn wall and note the arrows painted on it. The next stile leads to a narrow path leading down between hedgerows. Do not continue down it but take the stile in the left-hand hedge. This new path descends diagonally across the field to a stile at the side of a cottage. Take the drive at the side of the cottage to reach a road. Here turn left to where the road bends and then descend by the path with a handrail to an unsurfaced lane. This offers a quick way down to Ironbridge for walkers short of time.

More interesting is the final section down through Benthall Edge Woods again. A footpath sign points down a house drive. Walk along the drive in front of the stone house to a stile leading into woodland. A sign on the tree indicates the direction inside the wood. In 100 yards or so is a Woodland Trust dedication plate fixed to a wooden post. Shortly after, the path leaves the woodland, keeping to the line of the hedge to the next stile. The next field may carry an arable crop, in which case keep to the headland path near the hedge until a stile near a large oak gives access to Benthall Edge Woods.

The path leads downhill through a stand of holly trees. Keep right where other paths diverge and you will meet a short wooden rail fence which is on the Nature Trail. Turn right at the fence. The trail twists and turns, crosses two small streams and arrives at Post 7, marking a stand of wild service trees, an uncommon relative of the rowan. Considering the disturbance which has taken place here it is remarkable to find this species represented. Its presence usually indicates woodland which has remained undisturbed for a long period.

The descent now steepens, but log retaining steps have been provided and there is a handrail at Post 6. The task of route-finding now reduces to tracing back through the numbered waymark posts in descending order. However, a maze of alternative ways has appeared and it is easy to lose too much height and miss Posts 4 and 3. There is little chance of being lost: all ways down end on the railway walk which can be used to get back to Bower Yard and the start.

Walk 7
CAER CARADOC
SHROPSHIRE
5 miles

Caer Caradoc is the highest of the narrow hills which lie to the east of the small Shropshire town of Church Stretton. It is also the most rugged.

The rocks in this neighbourhood are some of the oldest in Britain, and this becomes more obvious as you climb the flanks of the hill. The rocks are hard and fine-grained, the result of being subjected to millions of years of heat, cold, and compression.

The summit was once home to the tribesmen of the Iron Age, and the ditches protecting their encampment can be traced, encircling the flat summit.

In clear weather Caradoc makes a good viewpoint, with the north Shropshire plain stretching into the distance. It is easy to imagine this flat land buried under a melting glacier, the ancient rocks underfoot protruding from the ice – the landscape of 100,000 years ago.

The walk begins at the Richard Robinson Playing Field in Church Stretton. The field lies opposite the end of Beaumont Road which leads off the north side of the main street. Early starters may be lucky enough to find a space in the small car park at the playing field entrance. The town's main car park lies to the south of the main street.

The craggy skyline of Caer Caradoc is unmistakable when seen across the field from near the main entrance. The hill further north is the Lawley. Walk diagonally across the field towards Caer Caradoc and look for a metal barrier roughly

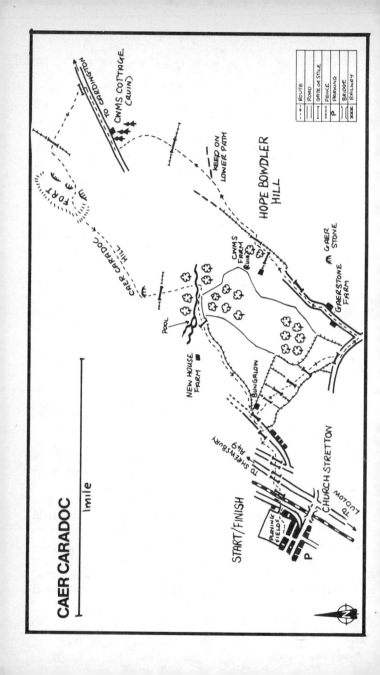

half-way along the boundary hedge. A footpath leads out of the field here and crosses a road, where it is signposted. The path continues behind Windsor Place to a stile at a railway crossing. Beyond the railway line cross a field to the A49.

Directly opposite across the A49 the path crosses a small field then an unsurfaced lane. The stiles in the hedgerows make the line of the path quite clear. In the field beyond the lane cross to the far hedge and follow it until a stile gives access to the lane leading to New House Farm. A cattle grid is placed across the lane at the farm drive. Note the public footpath sign pointing to Caer Caradoc; this path will be used on the return.

Cross a stile near the holly hedge bordering the garden of the white bungalow. Follow the line of the hedge then continue across a sequence of three stiles set in wire fences. The path has been gradually gaining height, so at the third stile spare a minute for the view. Long Mynd rises above Church Stretton and the Burway climbs steeply out of the town up Burway Hill. Gain a little more height to just beyond the solitary oak which stands in the field being crossed. Here the ridge of Caer Caradoc is seen end on.

The path skirts the wooded top of Helmeth Hill directly ahead. The next stile is placed in the corner of the field; across it, follow the right-hand fence to the Hope Bowdler road.

Follow the road uphill towards Hope Bowdler as far as the drive to Gaerstone Farm. The small crag from which the farm takes its name is a prominent landmark. The Gaer Stone, like the other outcrops hereabouts, is composed of some of the oldest rocks in Britain, at least 700 million years old.

Beyond Gaerstone Farm the stony bridleway ends at a field gate. The route now takes the rutted lane across the field to the ruins of Cwms Farm. The view of Caer Caradoc from near this point is the best of the walk. Cwms is a quiet secluded valley and Caradoc rises steeply out of it, the slopes covered with bracken, patches of gorse and small hawthorns.

At Cwms Farm the path leads out onto the rough grassland

The walk follows the quiet valley of Cwms which offers an attractive approach to the top of Caer Caradoc

of Hope Bowdler Hill. It runs, clearly defined, at a fairly constant level at the base of the hill. Continue through the wicket gate in the next fence and follow the path round to a small stand of pine trees near the ruins of Cwms Cottage. Here the path joins a wide stony track which was once the direct road from Cardington to Church Stretton. Follow the old road right, towards Cardington, to a stile at the starting point of the path to Caer Caradoc.

The whole of the hill was once rough grazing but the stile now leads into an area which has been enclosed and improved. There is a short very steep rise but once at the top the upper boundary fence comes into view. A stile adjacent to a tubular field gate gives access to a gently-graded path leading to the top of the hill. The width of the path and its even gradient are surely evidence that this was the way to the main entrance to the Iron Age fort.

The view northwards from Caer Caradoc is over the Lawley to the Wrekin, beyond which lies the flat plain of north Shropshire and Cheshire. Stapeley Hill projects from behind the northern end of the Long Mynd, and to its north rises Pontesford Hill. Beyond the Shropshire hills are the Briedden Hills near Welshpool, and, in clear weather, the Berwyns appear on the horizon. Closer at hand, and 800 feet below, Church Stretton sprawls across the flat valley floor.

An easy walk along the broad crest of the hill leads to Three Fingers Rock, and the ground now starts to drop steeply. A waymarked stile appears in a wire fence near a rock outcrop. Cross it and continue steeply down between clumps of gorse and stunted hawthorn to rejoin the old Cardington–Church Stretton road used earlier. Follow the old road now towards Church Stretton, going through a gate near New House Farm. The sunken overgrown track between the hedgerows, which was the original line of the road, has been abandoned. The path used now crosses the headland of the field, keeping close to the wire fence and eventually reaches the cattle grid on the New House Farm drive.

From here the first stage of the walk can be reversed to return to Church Stretton.

Walk 8
ST KENELM'S CHURCH
HEREFORD/WORCESTER
5¾ or 3¾ miles

St Kenelm's Church, at the north-eastern end of the Clent Hills, has a twelfth-century nave and chancel built in red sandstone. The western tower is a later, more ornate, structure in perpendicular style. The church stands alone some distance from the village, and this location is explained by an ancient legend. The tale is that Kenelm, son of a King of Mercia, was murdered here in 819AD at the command of his jealous sister. A holy spring arose from the ground where his body was found. The blocked arch in the south wall of the chancel is supposed to have a stairway behind leading down to the spring.

A window designed by Sir Edward Burne Jones in 1915, dedicated to child victims of the First World War, depicts scenes from Kenelm's life.

The walk starts from Sling Common to the south-east of the Clent Hills but it can also be joined from the Nimmings Visitor Centre on the north-west end for the shorter route. The Clent Hills are signposted from the A456 west of Halesowen via a lane which leads directly to the Nimmings Visitor Centre. Sling Common is best reached from the A491 which links the village of Hagley with junction 4 of the M5. On this approach, turn off the A491 at Hollies Hill along Gorse Green Lane. Sling Common is reached in half a mile. Park at the roadside by the pool.

Start along a drive, near a bye-laws noticeboard, which ends at a cottage. The path turns around the end of the

ST KENELM'S CHURCH

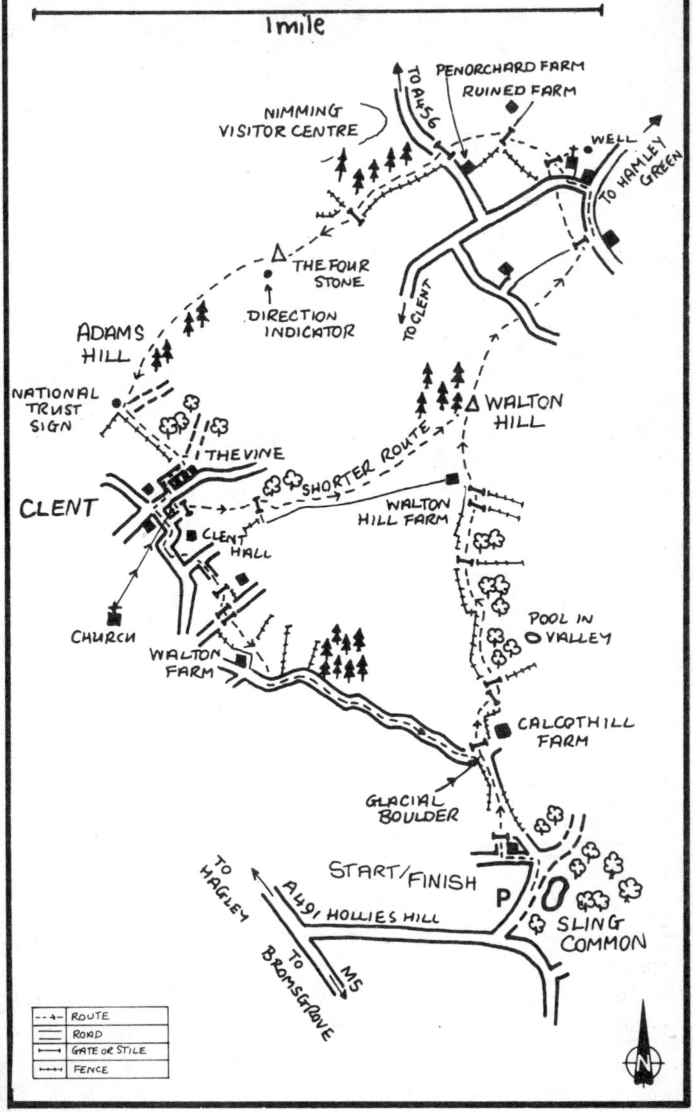

1 mile

TO PENORCHARD FARM
RUINED FARM
NIMMING VISITOR CENTRE
TO A456
WELL
TO HAMLEY GREEN

△ THE FOUR STONE
• DIRECTION INDICATOR

TO CLENT

ADAMS HILL

NATIONAL TRUST SIGN

THE VINE

SHORTER ROUTE

△ WALTON HILL

CLENT

WALTON HILL FARM

CLENT HALL

CHURCH

POOL IN VALLEY

WALTON FARM

CALCOTHILL FARM

GLACIAL BOULDER

START/FINISH

P

SLING COMMON

TO HAGLEY
A491 HOLLIES HILL
TO BROMSGROVE
M5

- - + -	ROUTE
	ROAD
	GATE OR STILE
	FENCE

cottage, passes through a gate and continues uphill to join the concrete drive leading to Calcothill Farm. On the left of the drive is a boulder transported by glacial ice from Arenig mountain near Bala in Wales. Next to the boulder is a stile. Cross, and follow the fence round to a further stile in the hedge on the right.

Cross the stile, and now the ground drops steeply away to the floor of the valley separating Walcot and Romsley Hill. The path now keeps to the line of the hedge and gradually gains height.

A stile in a wire fence is crossed and then the path winds round the head of a dry valley to three log seats by the path. Continue over the nearby stile in the wire fence. A waymarked post points to the left-hand hedge and the path keeps close to this, ending at a stile near a cottage. Cross the stile and the cottage drive where waymarks indicate the direction to the triangulation point on Walton Hill.

Walton Hill, at 1,033 feet, is the highest point on the walk. The most attractive distant views lie to the south and west. Northwards, the urban sprawl of the West Midlands towns masks much of the natural topography. Close at hand the wooded northern end of Clent Hill lies to the north-west.

A broad highway made by the passage of walkers and horseriders runs northwards from the triangulation point down to a car park on a narrow lane. On the last descent, avoid the main path and descend north-eastwards to a footpath sign on the opposite side of the lane. This points the way downhill across a large field to a stile in the corner. Cross this and follow the lane left to the turning to St Kenelm's Church.

Follow the signposted path to St Kenelm's Well, which now has been landscaped with a small network of terraced paths. A tablet has been placed on a wall behind the spring recording the legend.

To continue, cross the stile into the churchyard and walk round to the path approaching the western tower. A footpath starts from among the yew trees and leads to a stile in the hedge bordering the churchyard.

Cross the field to a leaning stump at the end of a broken

The tiny church of St Kenelm's, Clent is a plain building which is graced by an ornate 16th Century tower.

hedge and continue to a stile in the corner of the field. This lies at the edge of an old drive leading to the ruins of Penorchard Farm. The surface of the drive is not very good in wet weather; it becomes badly broken up and muddy.

Negotiate the drive uphill until it becomes possible to strike uphill across a field to a stile to the lane. The stile is almost opposite the entrance to Nimmings Visitor Centre. The path to the top of Clent Hill climbs up through the conifers and then across the open hill to the Four Stones, standing stones whose origins are uncertain. Continue westwards over the summit and then take a path which turns south through a wood and down to Clent village near the church.

Walkers who started from Nimmings Visitor Centre can complete the short walk by ascending Walton Hill directly from St Leonard's Church. The path follows the churchyard wall to a stile. It continues uphill across two fields to the edge of a small oak wood. Cross the stile into the wood where the way is quite clear – first it keeps to the line of a hedge and then crosses open hillside to the triangulation point.

Walkers returning to Sling Common must continue along the winding lane past Clent Hall. Just beyond the drive to Clent Hall Lodge (not the sort of building you would expect to have that name) a footpath runs diagonally across the field to a metal kissing gate. Go through the gate to the lane and walk down the drive of the house opposite. At the garden gate go right into the field, keep near the metal fence and cross a stile in the hedge. Cross into the lane and continue over the stile directly opposite. Cross the field to Walton Farm and then the field beyond to a stile in the hedge. Cross the stile into a wide unsurfaced lane.

The track is a public bridleway which twists and turns and ends after one mile at Calcothill Farm near the glacial boulder. The first stage of the walk can be retraced to Sling Common.

Walk 9
HARVINGTON HALL
HEREFORD/WORCESTER
8 miles

Worcestershire clays make fine red bricks that became virtually the universal building material of the county from the sixteenth century onwards. This local material has produced the lovely mellow exterior of Harvington Hall. Outwardly the house is Elizabethan, yet the main entrance is approached from a bridge over a moat more in character with earlier fortified houses. This gives a clue to one of the hall's surprises: the brick shell covers a much earlier medieval timber-framed building. The refacing and other additions were undertaken between 1560 and 1575.

Another surprising feature is that the hall is full of priest holes. There are few houses with quite as many ingeniously concealed hiding places as Harvington. The whereabouts of most of these are revealed to visitors making a tour of the house.

This walk, which will make a full day after allowing time to look over the hall, begins at the car park in the village of Blakedown on the A456 approximately two and a half miles east of Kidderminster. Begin along the Belbroughton road which leaves the A456 directly opposite the car park entrance. In quarter of a mile a sign at the end of semi-detached houses marks the beginning of a public bridleway which crosses a field to the tree-fringed Ladies Pool. Cross the earth bank dam and fork left to follow the edge of the pool round to converge on a wire fence. Follow this round the edge of a field to a stile on Sandy Lane.

HARVINGTON HALL

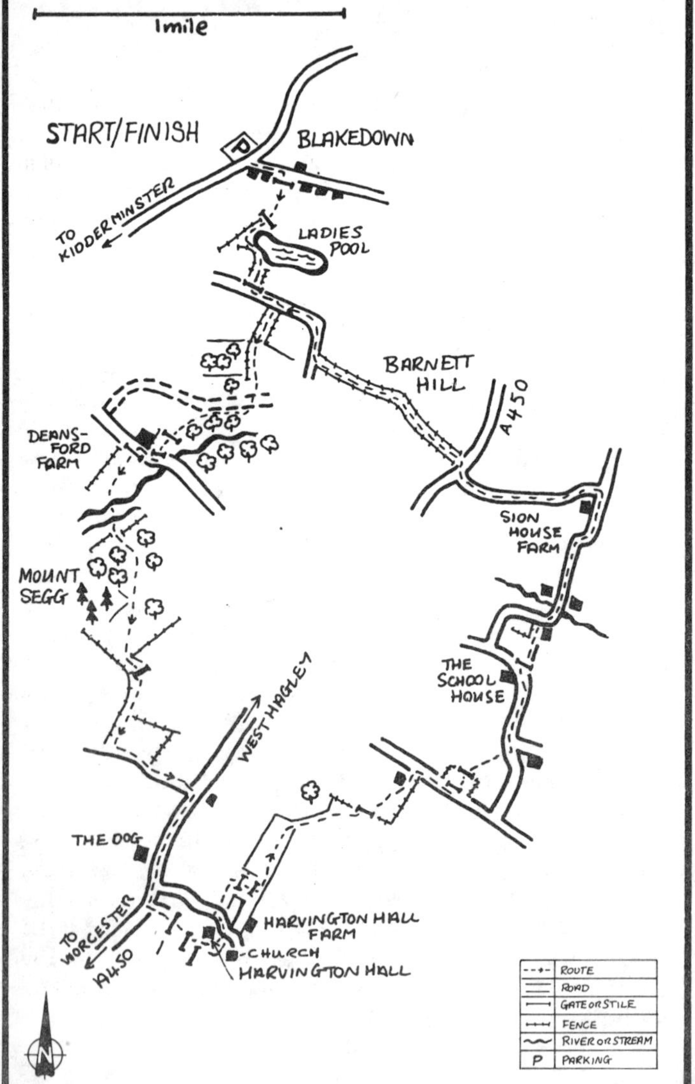

|← 1 mile →|

START/FINISH   **BLAKEDOWN**

TO KIDDERMINSTER

LADIES POOL

BARNETT HILL

A450

DEANS-FORD FARM

SION HOUSE FARM

MOUNT SEGG

THE SCHOOL HOUSE

WEST HAGLEY

THE DOG

TO WORCESTER

A450

HARVINGTON HALL FARM

CHURCH

HARVINGTON HALL

N

·-·+·-	ROUTE
——	ROAD
—|—	GATE OR STILE
++++	FENCE
～～	RIVER OR STREAM
P	PARKING

Turn left along the lane for 100 yards to a wide unsurfaced track which is signposted. The track leads uphill and runs along the eastern side of a small wood. Beyond the wood the path descends to a solitary oak by a farm access track. Continue downhill to the edge of the wood and follow this, to the right, to an electricity pylon near the farm buildings. Go over a stile into the next field; cross to a stile with the usual signpost in the lane.

Opposite Deansford Farm a sign marks the beginning of a bridleway to a wooded knoll, Mount Segg. The true line of the bridleway is due south across the field to a bridge at the first stream. Local horseriders prefer the farm access track which first skirts the field and then turns sharply across it to the bridge. The track is wide and obvious and it continues across a second bridge and enters woodland on the slopes of Mount Segg.

Where the woodland changes to planted conifers, break left along a wide sandy path leading gradually uphill through bracken. At the top of the rise there is a wide open view across fields to the distant Abberley Hills and the Titterstone Clee. Now fork right to a wicket gate and keep to a headland path across two fields to a wide farm track leading to the A450.

The lane leading to Harvington Hall is signposted on the A450 but a preferable way for the walker starts along the drive between Steppe Farm and a cottage. At a bend take to the field, keeping near the hedge. The next stile leads into a field with a landscaped pool and the lovely setting of the hall becomes more apparent. A final gate near the entrance to the hall car park leads to the open space in front of the hall where a footbridge across the moat leads to the entrance.

To continue the walk follow the lane round the moat towards Harvington village. At the bend in the road take the field gate on the left and follow the obvious farm track along the line of the hedge. At the end of the hedge turn right along the line indicated by a waymarker to a stile. Cross into the next field and on to a second stile to a grassy lane. In 100 yards the lane opens into a long narrow field with a headland path running along its length.

A medieval moat still protects the courtyard entrance of Harvington Hall

At the field end cross through the gap in the hedge and follow the headland round to a small triangular area of newly planted trees. The spire of the church at Chaddesley Corbett is a prominent landmark. Follow the obvious track through trees to the next field; cross diagonally downhill and through the far edge to a gate near Woodrow Nursery. The plastic tunnel greenhouses of the nursery are clearly visible and confirm the direction to be followed. A lane leads from the gate to the road at Woodrow.

Turn right along the road for 100 yards, cross the stile in the hedge on the left side of the road into a field. Directly ahead are the Clent Hills which add interest to otherwise flat countryside. A further stile gives access to a large arable field where the path leads directly across to the lane at Woodhouse Farm. Follow the lane to the left for quarter of a mile to School House. Opposite the house a stile marks the beginning of a path which follows the line of the hedge and ends on the drive of a renovated cottage at Hill Pool.

Turn right at the lane; it crosses a stream and then gradually climbs uphill for half a mile to Sion House Farm. A public bridleway leaves the lane here, through the farm yard and keeping a straight course between retaining walls and hedgerows to the lodge gate of Sion House. Follow the drive from the lodge of the A450.

Directly across the A450 a bridleway leads uphill over Barnett Hill to New Wood Lane. This is the highest point of the walk and the path along the top of the hill provides extensive views of the surrounding countryside. Easily recognisable landmarks are the Malvern Hills (south), Abberley Hills (south-west), Titterstone Clee and Brown Clee (north-west) and the Clent Hills (north-east).

The bridleway over Barnett Hill ends on the lane quarter of a mile from the path skirting Ladies Pool used at the start of the walk. Retrace this section back to the car park at Blakedown.

Walk 10
SEVERN VALLEY RAILWAY
HEREFORD/WORCESTER
8 miles

British Rail ceased operating the Severn Valley line in 1970 and that might have been the end of the railway but for the group of steam locomotive enthusiasts who founded the Severn Valley Railway Company.

The company re-opened the line from Bridgnorth to Bewdley in 1974, and now the railway has become an important tourist attraction. This success led to the company re-opening the old line from Bewdley to Kidderminster, providing a link with British Rail trains.

The most scenic section of the line follows the course of the River Severn for 12¾ miles from Bridgnorth to Bewdley. In this tranquil setting the sight of the ex-Great Western Railway Hall or Manor Class 4–6–0 locomotives hauling the trains recreates the atmosphere of the 1930s.

This section of the line also has several bridges and viaducts which are monuments to the skill of Victorian engineers. The most impressive is the Victoria Bridge which carries the line over the Severn on a single arch with a span of 200 feet.

Trains run at weekends from March to October. In Bank Holiday weeks and the peak holiday times in summer a daily service operates.

This walk could be combined with a ride on the train from Bewdley to Arley, walking back along the west bank of the Severn, halving the distance walked.

Begin at the main car park north of the High Street in

SEVERN VALLEY RAILWAY

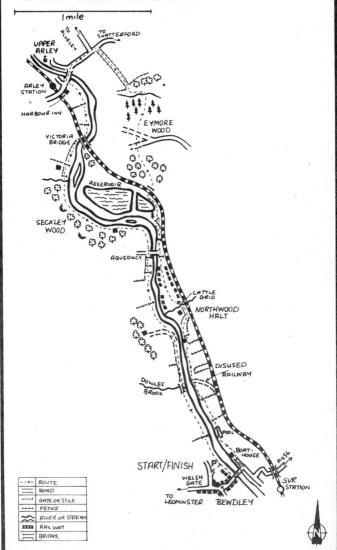

1 mile

TO BLVELEY
TO SHATTERFORD

UPPER ARLEY

ARLEY STATION

HARBOUR INN

EYMORE WOOD

VICTORIA BRIDGE

RESERVOIR

SECKLEY WOOD

AQUEDUCT

CATTLE GRID

NORTHWOOD HALT

DISUSED RAILWAY

DOWLES BROOK

POOL

BOAT HOUSE

A456

START/FINISH

P

WELSH GATE

SVR STATION

TO LEOMINSTER

BEWDLEY

--·+-	ROUTE
	ROAD
	GATE OR STILE
·····→	FENCE
~~	RIVER OR STREAM
▥▥▥	RAILWAY
	BRIDGE

N

Bewdley, reached from the B4363 which leaves the A456 at Welch Gate on the road out of the town.

Join the riverside walk opposite the boathouse of the Bewdley Rowing Club. A gravel path continues for half a mile then a footbridge crosses Dowles Brook near remains of an old railway bridge which carried the old GWR branch line across the river.

A wide cinder track now continues on the riverside, passing an old cottage, with a half-timbered gable end, which featured in a series of coloured prints of Midland scenes by the Birmingham artist James Priddy.

In half a mile the cinder track turns away from the river and runs to a cottage at the edge of woodland. Leave the track and continue on the bank across a field to go over a stile. Two wicket gates lead to the aqueduct over the river which carries Birmingham's water from the Elan Valley reservoirs in Mid-Wales.

The footpath now rounds Folly Point and enters Seckley Wood. The ground falls steeply to the river and bands of buff-coloured shaly rock outcrop on the sloping bank. They are part of the coal measures strata from which coal was once mined higher up the river at Highley and in the Wyre Forest.

The wood ends at a small stream and the path crosses two meadows to reach Victoria Bridge. The railway line loops away through a cutting before reaching Arley Station. The riverside path crosses three fields before reaching the village. There used to be a ferry crossing at Upper Arley, and the landing stages can still be seen on either bank. Now the river is crossed in dull fashion by a tubular steel footbridge.

Cross the bridge and continue by road towards Shatterford, uphill out of the village, passing the school, memorial hall, and the side turn to Alveley. A Victorian house on the right has a tall yew hedge protecting its front garden. Immediately at the end of the hedge begins a bridleway.

The bridleway follows a wide grassy lane which finally enters Eymore Wood. This was once a continuation of the Wyre Forest but today much of the old natural forest has been cleared to make way for conifers. A short stretch of the

Robert Kirk

The Victoria Bridge is a fine example of 19th Century railway engineering

old natural forest of oak, birch, and holly remains on the edge where the bridleway enters the wood and crosses a stream. From the stream a wide forestry extraction road climbs uphill through a stand of larches and continues on a gentle descent through evergreen conifers of mixed variety. Keep straight ahead at the crossing with another extraction road and in quarter of a mile is a gate opening onto the surfaced lane leading to Trimpley Reservoir.

Across the lane a signposted footpath leads down through deciduous woodland to the railway line near the reservoirs. Cross the line and walk round the eastern end of the small reservoir to a shelter belt of pine trees. At this point descend to the river bank to a stile in an overgrown hedge. Cross the stile and follow the path in front of some holiday chalets to a brick cottage.

From here the path follows a stony drive to the Birmingham aqueduct, and a gate marks the extent of the corporation's property. On the right of the gate is a stile. Cross into the field along the fences which cordon off the riverside chalets. The path now crosses a stream and roughly follows an electricity power line. There is a rash of chalets and eventually a stream bars further progress.

Escape from the field over a cattlegrid to the lane. (A telephone kiosk marks the end of a drive which leads up to Northwood Halt on the SVR line). Continue south on the lane for 200 yards. A close-boarded fence guards the roadside frontage of the large property on the right. At the end of the fence a drive leads to the forecourt of Eversley Bungalow. Follow the drive to the bungalow and then cross the stile into the field. Make for the river bank by crossing a metal hurdle at a gap in the next hedge.

The path now follows the eastern bank of the river back to Bewdley. There are no difficulties and there is a clear path to the rowing club boathouse. Here cross to an unsurfaced lane which ends at the bridge in Bewdley. A final point of interest to note as the bridge is crossed: moored at Severnside North, a little way upstream, is the old Arley ferryboat. It is now used as a landing stage for the hire of dinghies.

Walk 11
WITLEY COURT
HEREFORD/WORCESTER
7½ or 5½ miles

Witley Court, once a symbol of Victorian wealth and patronage, was destroyed by fire in 1937, but even the shell which remains is impressive. The Victorian palace was built on the site of a Jacobean house and chapel. Luckily the chapel escaped damage from the fire, and is the real point of interest on this walk.

The brick chapel was faced with ashlar masonry during Victorian reconstruction, but the interior is in the ornate late baroque style of 100 years earlier. The interior treatment was described by Pevsner as the most 'Italian ecclesiastical space in the whole of England'. The wall panels and coving are finished in white and gold, and the ceiling is decorated with paintings by Antonio Bellucci, an Italian painter who came to England in 1716. The paintings and the painted glass in the windows were brought here from the Duke of Chandos' mansion at Canons near Edgware in 1747.

The walk starts from the A451 one mile east of Great Witley. The north-west verge of the road is suitable for parking. The starting point is marked by footpath signs on either side of the road: one runs north-west to Abberley Hill; the other, south-east to Hillhampton, which you take.

Follow the drive to Hill House Farm. The path bends sharply round the outbuildings and continues through the metal field gate near a small pool. The path, confined between fences and hedgerows, ends at a gate near a corrugated iron barn.

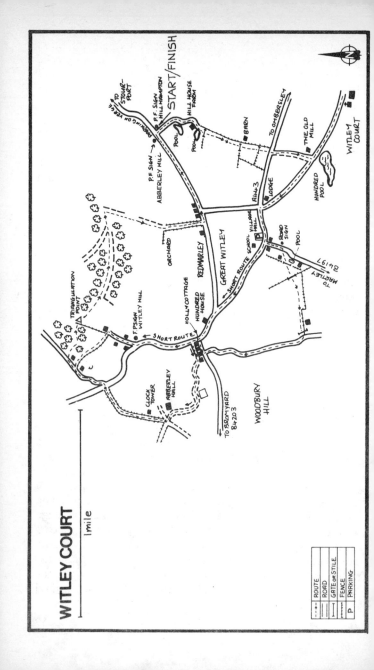

WITLEY COURT

1 mile

ROUTE
ROAD
GATE or STILE
FENCE
P PARKING

START/FINISH

TO STOURPORT

P.F. SIGN HILL HAMPTON

HILL HOUSE FARM

PARKING ON VERGE

POOL

P.F. SIGN ABBERLEY HILL

POOL

POOL

BARN

TO OMBERSLEY

THE OLD MILL

WITLEY COURT

A.H.-3

LODGE

HUNDRED POOL

ORCHARD

REDMARLEY

GREAT WITLEY

VILLAGE HALL

SHORT ROUTE

SCHOOL

ROAD SIGN

POOL

TRIANGULATION POINT

F.P. SIGN WITLEY HILL

SHORT ROUTE

HOLLY COTTAGE

HUNDRED HOUSE

B4197

TO MARTLEY

CLOCK TOWER

ABBERLEY HALL

TO BROMYARD B4203

WOODBURY HILL

Beyond the barn the path continues in the same direction across two fields to the A443. Directly opposite across the road is a wide unsurfaced track on which walkers and horseriders have de facto rights of access. It leads to the main drive to Witley Court at Hundred Pool – turn left.

From the court, retrace the length of the drive to Hundred Pool and continue to the lodge at the main road. Turn left on the A443 for 300 yards to the T-junction with the B4197.

The shorter walk can be taken here by using the roadside footpath to the Hundred House Inn. Continue on the main road along a footpath to the start of the path up Witley Hill. The path to the top is signposted up the steep and narrow lane. When progress is barred by the drive of a cottage, follow the Country Landowner's Association waymark signs to a stile leading into pasture. The path keeps to the line of the left-hand hedge and ends on Wynniats Way, a narrow lane leading to Abberley Village. To continue pick up the reference to Wynniats Way in the description of the full walk.

A quieter and more pleasant alternative to this main road diversion can be found. It crosses fields and runs through the grounds of Abberley Hall. Take the B4197 Martley road for 150 yards. Opposite a road sign is the drive of a house which is also the start of a footpath. The path leaves the drive and passes near a small pool to a gate. There may be cattle-churned mud to negotiate at the gate where the stream enters the pool but beyond this point the going improves. Cross the field to a double stile in the hedge due west of the pool. The path keeps on a westerly line across a large field ending at a stile leading into a narrow quiet lane.

Turn northwards along the lane to the B4203 then right to the A443. The house on the corner at the T-junction is The Old Bakery. A few yards uphill on the A443 is Holly Cottage where a path begins. Behind Holly Cottage a wide tractor track leads through the woods to a locked gate. Use the stile at the side of the gate and continue to where the track forks. Keep left here passing a small pool. Beyond this point the track through the woods bends sharp right, then left, around

At Witley Court the fine Baroque Church is still joined to the ruins of the former mansion

farm buildings. The track then turns uphill passing near a small quarry screened with rhododendrons and finally arrives at Abberley Hall.

Abberley Hall was built in 1846 and is now used as a public school. Beyond the hall is a meeting of four ways. Two are marked private, and our route takes the unsurfaced track running roughly northwards which bisects these two. The track is bounded on the west by a six-foot high wire fence but beyond it are good views up the Teme valley. The track also passes close by the foot of the tall clock tower which is such a dominant landmark. The tower once earned the name of Jones Folly, for it was built by John Joseph Jones in 1883 in memory of his father, the original owner of the Hall.

Wynniats Way lies directly opposite the end of this track at the A443. Follow the way, which is a narrow lane, passing the short-route footpath described earlier which comes up from Great Witley. Take the next footpath, signposted Redmarley; it winds uphill through coppiced saplings of oak and beech and sycamore to the triangulation point on the summit. Here the southerly aspect opens up to Woodbury Hill and beyond.

A clearly defined path now winds eastwards along the crest of the hill and enters woodland. It is difficult on first acquaintance with the hill to find the start of the paths leading off to the south. The easiest to find is the bridleway leading to Redmarley. The path along the crest descends through woodland to where a clear track comes up on the left side from Abberley village.

The bridleway to Redmarley starts 300 yards beyond this point just over the next rise. Look for a grassy line leading south through the bracken and for the remains of a chestnut fence. The line becomes clearer as you descend, running steeply down a spur separating two bracken-infested valleys. The fence reappears to confirm the direction as the path descends through a coppice. Finally the path enters a sunken lane, with orchards on either hand, to end on the A451. A half-mile of footpath on the roadside verge leads to the start of the walk.

Walk 12
CROFT CASTLE
HEREFORD/WORCESTER
$4\frac{1}{2}$ miles

Croft Castle, five miles north-west of Leominster, was an important stronghold guarding the Welsh border and is mentioned in the Domesday Book. Except for a brief period in the reign of George III, the castle has been the home of the Croft family since the time of Edward the Confessor.

The building is impressive. The circular towers and oldest parts of the walls date from the fourteenth and fifteenth centuries. In later more peaceful times the fortifications were removed and the castle was rebuilt into a large country house. Eighteenth-century additions in Georgian style and later nineteenth-century Gothic Revival extensions have created an austere symmetrical exterior.

Close by (and very small compared to the large house) is the church of St Michael and All Angels.

The castle is now owned by the National Trust. Opening times: April and October, weekends only (and Easter Monday), 2pm – 5pm; May to September, Wednesday to Sunday (and Bank Holiday Monday), 2pm – 6pm.

The walk starts on Bircher Common, an area of open grassland managed by the National Trust, lying just north of the B4362 eight miles south-west of Ludlow. A narrow lane leads onto the common at a cross roads by a war memorial half a mile east of Cock Gate and half a mile west of the village of Bircher. The lane ends at a cattle grid and thereafter a rough track leads across the common where it is possible to park on either side.

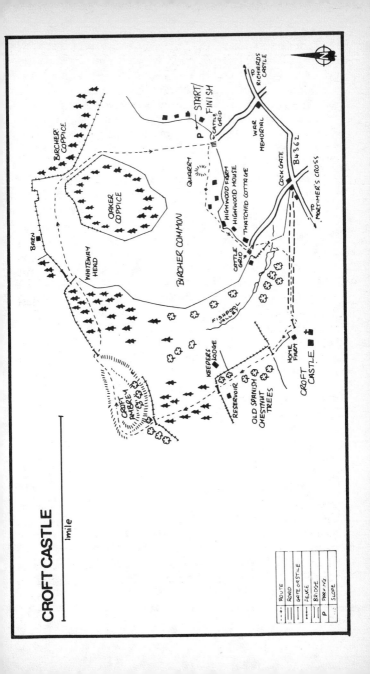

CROFT CASTLE

1mile

····	ROUTE
	ROAD
	GATE OR STILE
	FENCE
	BRIDGE
P	PARKING
···	SLOPE

Small stone cottages and farmhouses are scattered around the edge of the common. A small overgrown quarry and other evidence of disturbance of the ground identify the source of the building material and also the nature of the underlying rock. The Silurian limestones and shales which give rise to the distinctive scenery of Wenlock Edge outcrop again here. The rocks produce a landscape of round wooded hills which fall steeply away to the north-west. To the south-east the rocks slope at a more gentle angle.

The lower end of the common is crossed by a maze of sheep tracks leading through the bracken. Take the widest to be found and aim to work around the northern side of the commoners' cottages. Soon a wide unsurfaced track is met; this leads past Highwood House to the end of the lane from Cock Gate.

There is a beautiful half-timbered cottage with a thatched roof at the lane end, and opposite it a stile marks the start of a footpath leading diagonally downhill across a field. A stile set in a wire fence continues the line downhill through woodland to a grass-covered bank which dams the lowest of the series of pools in Fishpool Valley. Cross the dam and climb the grassy slope beyond to the drive which leads to the entrance of Croft Castle.

The drive is shaded throughout its length of just over half a mile by magnificent tall oak trees. Continue from the gate-house to the castle. Several waymarked trails have been laid out in the Croft Castle estate for visitors. The routes are shown on a display board on one of the wide grass verges used as a parking space. The path to Croft Ambrey, the next objective, starts from the field gate near the display board. It begins along a farm track which winds round the north side of the Croft Home Farm buildings. The path gradually gains height and passes through another gate.

A line of sweet chestnut trees lies to the west of the path at this point. The fissures in the lower parts of the trunks form a distinctive flat spiral, and this characteristic, plus the massive girth of the trunks, indicate their considerable age – over 350 years. They are reputed to have been grown from

At Croft Castle the severe lines of a medieval tower make a visual contrast with the shapely cupola of the church

chestnuts salvaged from one of the ships of the Spanish Armada which was wrecked off the coast of Wales.

The slope eases off as the path approaches a conifer plantation and there is an extensive view across Herefordshire. The Abberley Hills near Great Witley are due east, and to the south-east the unmistakable outline of the Malvern Hills can usually be seen against the hazy outline of the northern end of the Cotswolds. Fine specimens of oak and chestnut border one side of the path, from which it is possible to return by a path which descends into Fishpool Valley from near the Keeper's Lodge. This route descends through attractive woodland but it is frequently muddy underfoot.

The path to Croft Ambrey hill fort runs on through the conifer plantation emerging from it near the outer ditches of the fort. The path first keeps to the crest of the escarpment and finally turns through a break in the ramparts into the hill fort. This holds a commanding position, with the ground falling away steeply to the north and west, opening up views of the Radnor forest. In a more northerly direction the hills of the Clun forest rise beyond the valley of the River Teme.

The size and extent of the earthworks at Croft Ambrey are impressive. The camp was occupied from about 550BC to 50AD and it held a population of between 500 and 900.

The path leaves Croft Ambrey by descending the eastern embankment into woodland. A wicket gate leads into a conifer plantation to link with the broad green track leading to Whiteway Head. Two other paths lead downhill from the wicket gate, one into Fishpool Valley and the second to the Keeper's Lodge referred to earlier. The direction of the path to Whiteway Head is north-east and it maintains height.

At Whiteway Head the open grassy common is crossed to the northern edge of Oaker Coppice. Here a wide track follows the edge of the coppice to break out into the open common again at a lower level, but there is still sufficient elevation to give a fine prospect of Titterstone Clee and the neighbouring Brown Clee to the north.

Having enjoyed this last view the final stretch of the common is all descent to the starting point.

Walk 13
HEREFORDSHIRE BEACON & MIDSUMMER HILL
HEREFORD/WORCESTER
6 miles

Two of the Malvern Hills at the southern end of the range are topped by impressive Iron Age hill forts. The higher of the two, on Herefordshire Beacon, lies at just over 1,000 feet above sea level. The original embankment here enclosed seven acres and had entrances at the four cardinal points of the compass. Later defences enclosed roughly 19 acres of habitable land, and the size of the encampment suggests that it was an important settlement. Much later the Normans recognised the defensive value of the site and built a ringwork inside the old earthworks on the highest point.

Roughly two miles south of Herefordshire Beacon is Midsummer Hill Camp where a single rampart and ditch encloses 19 acres on the tops of twin hills. Excavations revealed lines of back-to-back houses of rectangular plan. Assuming that the dwellings were used for accommodation then the old idea of Iron Age people living as herdsmen penning animals inside the ramparts has to be abandoned. It appears people lived close together in these camps and were arable farmers. Certainly Midsummer Hill was continuously occupied for over 500 years before the Roman conquest of Britain.

Begin from Castlemorton Common, near the southern end of the Malvern Hills, reached by turning south from the A4104 at Welland. One mile south of Welland on the B4208 a minor unsurfaced road runs across the common to the old quarry at the Gullet. Cars may be parked at the side of this minor road at several places.

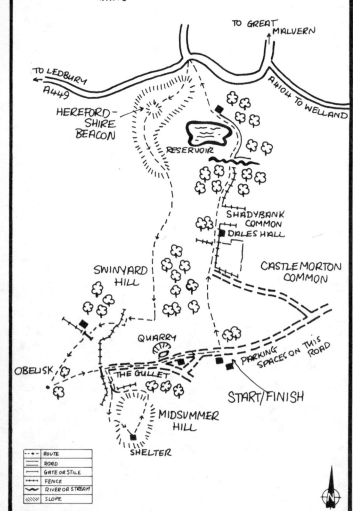

HEREFORDSHIRE BEACON
AND MIDSUMMER HILL

| | 1mile | |

TO GREAT MALVERN

TO LEDBURY
A449

A4104 TO WELLAND

HEREFORD-
SHIRE
BEACON

RESERVOIR

SHADYBANK
COMMON

DALES HALL

CASTLEMORTON
COMMON

SWINYARD
HILL

QUARRY

PARKING SPACES ON THIS ROAD

OBELISK

THE GULLET

START/FINISH

MIDSUMMER
HILL

SHELTER

- - + - -	ROUTE
═══	ROAD
—⊢—	GATE OR STILE
+++	FENCE
∿	RIVER OR STREAM
▨▨▨	SLOPE

N

You can wander freely across the open common and the place is popular in summer for family outings and picnics.

A bridleway starts from the road roughly quarter of a mile from the turning to Chandlers Cross. Two farm buildings lie to the south of the road and opposite are a group of pollarded willows and a weedy pool. The bridleway can be traced across the common both by signs of use and by the line of an old low embankment.

The bridleway crosses the common to the south-west corner of a wood and joins an unsurfaced road to Dales Hall. A track continues from the hall across Shadybank Common but beyond the hall a path forks left passing under a power line. Ignore the footpath going steeply uphill, signposted No Horseriding, and continue on the bridleway. This follows a more level course alongside a hedge and runs on through open new woodland. Continue through more mature woodland where leaf litter keeps down growth on the ground and makes the path even more distinct. Cross a stream at the head of a steep-sided valley and climb beside a stone wall to the British Camp reservoir. A surfaced drive leads from here to the car park at Wynds Point on the A4104.

The path from the car park to the top of Herefordshire Beacon is surfaced, making the climb rather tame, but it is interesting to trace the lines of the earthworks which contour the hill at different levels.

The view from the top of Herefordshire Beacon is extensive and fully repays the effort expended in reaching it. Continue along the crest of the hill to the southern end of the highest ramparts. Here a path surfaced with stone leads down to a direction indicator offering a choice of routes. Use either the route over Hangman's Hill, which keeps to the crest of the ridge, or one which keeps to a lower level on the western side leading to Clutters Cave.

Beyond Clutters Cave the lower path rejoins the path on the crest to follow the line of the Shire Ditch, an earthwork which runs the full length of the Malvern Hills. It dates from 1283 and was constructed to distinguish lands owned by the Earls of Gloucester from those of the Bishops of Hereford.

The top of Hereford Beacon is dissected by an elaborate network of embankments and ditches

The Shire Ditch marks the way over Swinyard Hill to a direction indicator. It is possible to shorten the walk from this point by following the arrow to Castlemorton Common, so avoiding Midsummer Hill. But if time allows, it is worth the extra distance.

The arrow for Midsummer Hill on the indicator points westward and the path runs downhill to join a wide unsurfaced track. Follow the track southwards through woodland to a sharp left-hand bend. Here a stile and gate give access to a path leading through a coppice. Follow the path through a gate near a cottage. It now continues across grassland of the Deer Park to the huge obelisk which is less than half a mile away.

The obelisk was erected in memory of John Lord Somers, Baron of Evesham, and his descendants. The inscriptions on the four faces of the obelisk tell the story in more detail. Here is a good place from which to look back at the Herefordshire Beacon and survey the route we have followed. The earthworks on Midsummer Hill, the next objective, can also be clearly seen.

Midsummer Hill is reached by following the wide track leading eastwards to a gate. Continuing this direction will lead downhill to the quarry at the Gullet, but southwards a track leads gradually uphill between wire fences to a point where it becomes possible to scramble upwards over steep open ground to the top of Midsummer Hill. Towards the southern end of the old fort is a stone shelter looking out over the Severn valley.

It is worth making a circuit of the embankments which girdle the hill before returning to the starting point. The most direct way back is to pick up a path which comes into the fort at the old northern entrance. This winds round to rejoin the wide track used on the way up. Return to the head of the Gullet and then descend to the quarry. The quarry face has a pool at its base and the path on the old spoil-heap alongside joins the road to Castlemorton at a cottage. Continue along the road to where your car is parked.

Walk 14
BROADWAY TOWER
HEREFORD/WORCESTER
4½ miles

The Cotswold escarpment approaches its northern limit at Broadway and the steep high hill above the village is a magnificent vantage point. The view is over the Avon and Severn valleys and extends westwards to the Welsh border.

In 1800 the Earl of Coventry built a folly on Broadway Hill, presumably to take advantage of this fine view. The folly, a stone tower placed near the steep edge of the escarpment, makes a prominent landmark. The tower is a fanciful creation, a hexagonal prism set on end with circular towers placed at three of the vertexes. Rounded arches to the windows revive the Norman practice. The tower seems to symbolise the romanticism which affected early nineteenth-century taste in landscape and which took classical as well as medieval forms.

The land around the tower is now managed as a country park and there is much to see. Walkers preoccupied with the view, which is particularly good when the afternoon sun brings the Malverns and the Welsh Border Hills into sharp relief, can gain a little extra height by looking at it from the battlements of the tower. For a small fee, of course.

This walk begins in the Worcestershire village of Broadway, on the A44 six miles from Evesham. The houses in the main street of the village, made entirely of honey-coloured Cotswold stone and decked with grass verges, create a timeless atmosphere which is almost too good to be true. The village is a heart of England showplace and it has been

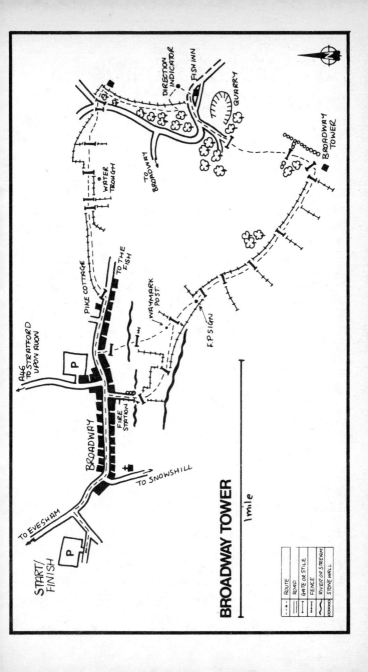

BROADWAY TOWER

1 mile

	ROUTE
	ROAD
	GATE OR STILE
	FENCE
	RIVER OR STREAM
	STONE WALL

START/FINISH

TO EVESHAM

A46 TO STRATFORD UPON AVON

P

BROADWAY

TO SNOWSHILL

FIRE STATION

PIKE COTTAGE

TO THE FISH

WATER TROUGH

WAYMARK POST

F.P SIGN

TO BROADWAY

DIRECTION INDICATOR

FISH INN

QUARRY

BROADWAY TOWER

carefully preserved with precise attention to detail.

The walk can be started from either of two car parks shown on the map and there is also a car park and picnic site on Fish Hill at the mid-point of the walk.

The description starts from the main village street which is followed to its end. By the last building on the left, Pike Cottage, is a stile and a footpath sign pointing to Chipping Campden. The path climbs uphill, keeping beside a rail fence, to a stile at the top end of a green lane. Opposite is a wicket gate giving access to the next field. Continue along the field boundary on the right to a metal wicket gate. The path across the next field passes close to a watering trough fed from a spring and beyond it is a stile set in the hedge. Cross the stile and continue uphill to a stile and field gate at a road.

Cross the road and take the path signposted to Fish Hill. A line of steps eases the climb up the steep slope of the escarpment. Near the crest the path keeps to a fairly level course through a beech wood. The wood has been replanted in part with larches but it still retains some fine old trees. A group of three tall beeches occupies a clearing from where there is an extensive view north-eastwards across the vale of Evesham.

The path continues through a tangled coppice and down a line of steps into an old quarry. There are a few false trails running between the old spoilheaps to be avoided. The correct path climbs steeply out of the quarry up a flight of steps and then crosses to the toposcope at the picnic site on Fish Hill.

The Cotswold Way Long Distance Path passes near the toposcope, and this walk now uses a section of it. Follow the Cotswold Way signpost to the road near the Fish Inn, cross the road and find the old quarry road which starts on the left a little way down the hill towards Broadway. The neighbourhood of the quarry is unsightly but is soon passed and the stony track turns through woodland to a stile. Cross the stile and break out of the wood into pasture.

Ahead are grassy embankments which have a prehistoric look, but their origins are more modern – they are the healed

Broadway Tower stands on a prominent hill near the northern end of the Cotswolds

scars of former quarry workings. After negotiating the embankments, Broadway Tower should be in sight. The path keeps near the stone wall on the left and goes through a field gate to the boundary fence of Broadway Country Park and beside the tower.

It is easy to see why the tower is such a prominent landmark. It stands at an altitude of over 1,000 feet, and the nearest land of comparable height is on the Malvern Hills to the west and the Clent Hills to the north. On a clear day the views are marvellous, with the towers of Worcester Cathedral, Warwick Castle, Tewkesbury Abbey, and the spire of Coventry Cathedral all reputed to be visible.

The footpath goes through the wicket gate into the park and immediately turns right along the fence to another wicket. This is all a continuation of the Cotswold Way, and the path descends along the line of the fence over a succession of waymarked stiles. It is all straightforward easy walking which allows the enjoyment of the views ahead. The rounded lump of Bredon Hill lies ahead, a mass of Cotswold limestone which has become detached from the main bulk of the escarpment. On the other side of it the River Avon flows south from Pershore to flow into the Severn at Tewkesbury.

The fence which has been our direction indicator for the last half a mile ends at a gate. Near it is a footpath sign pointing to Broadway. Continue downhill across the field to a stile, cross, and pick up the faint line of a sunken track. A waymark post here offers a choice. The Cotswold Way diverts diagonally across the field to reach the upper end of the main street in Broadway. The path ahead keeps green fields underfoot for a little longer and makes a better finish on this outing.

Continue downhill to the green corrugated iron shed near the stream and through the gate beyond. Cross the next field and in the right-hand corner is a stile adjacent to the field gate. From here a drive leads to the main street, passing the fire station entrance. The drive ends almost opposite where the A46 Stratford-upon-Avon road leaves the main street of this delightful village.

Walk 15
BROOMBRIGGS FARM TRAIL
LEICESTERSHIRE
6 or 5 miles

Broombriggs, a mixed arable and stock farm of 139 acres in the Charnwood Forest, was presented to the Leicestershire County Council in 1970. It is tenanted on a commercial basis and is very much a working farm. The County Council have waymarked a farm trail approximately one and a half miles in length with a picnic site near the half-way point.

Information boards have been placed at intervals along the trail to explain the working operations of the farm, what varieties of crops are being grown, and pinpoint features of interest in the surrounding landscape. The trail boards are in place from April to October and are changed from time to time, but the paths are open throughout the year during daylight hours. There is no charge for walking the trail but there is a small one for cars parked at the trail car park.

You begin your walk at Beacon Hill, one of the highest points in Leicestershire. There are two car parks which would serve as starting points: Beacon Hill upper car park is close to the top of the hill and is reached from the B591 Copt Oak to Woodhouse Eaves road. The lower car park lies alongside the Woodhouse Eaves to Nanpanton Road and is crossed during the early part of the walk. There is also a car park which specifically serves the Broombriggs Farm Trail.

The route is described as starting from the upper car park, from where it is only a short walk between small outcrops of rock to the triangulation point at the top. The view is spectacular and a toposcope has been placed nearby to help

BROOMBRIGGS FARM

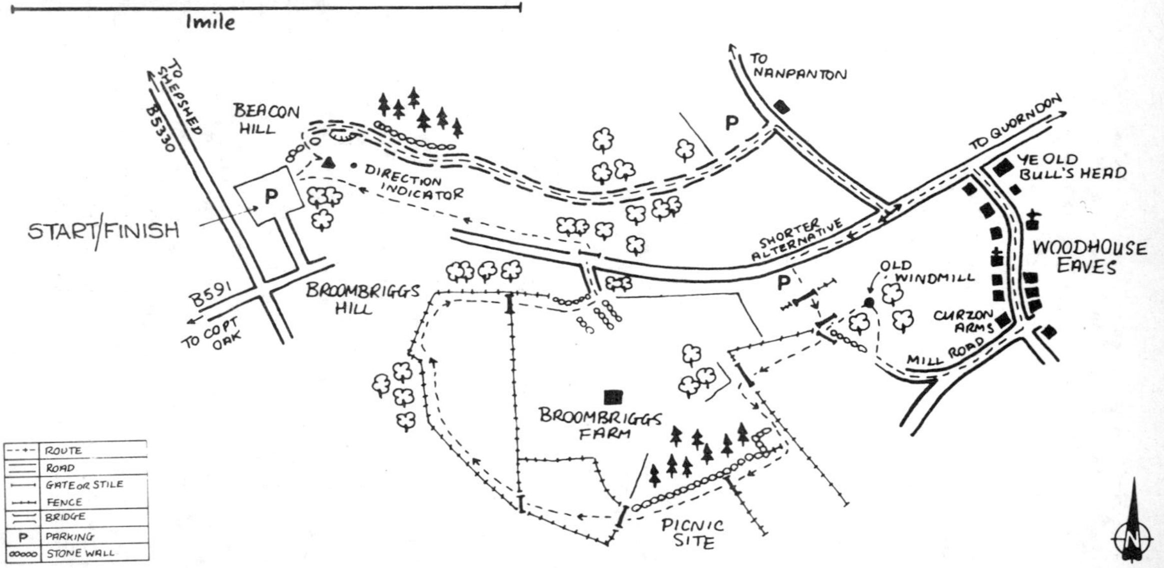

|—————| 1 mile

	ROUTE
	ROAD
	GATE or STILE
	FENCE
	BRIDGE
P	PARKING
	STONE WALL

TO GUORNDON

YE OLD BULL'S HEAD

WOODHOUSE EAVES

CURZON ARMS

MILL ROAD

OLD WINDMILL

TO NANPANTON

SHORTER ALTERNATIVE

P

P

P

PICNIC SITE

BROOMBRIGGS FARM

DIRECTION INDICATOR

BEACON HILL

BROOMBRIGGS HILL

TO SHEPSHED

B5330

B591

COPT TO OAK

START/FINISH

identify distant landmarks. To the south the Old John Tower will be immediately recognised by readers who have followed the Bradgate House walk.

Charnwood Forest presents a landscape of contrasts. On the high ground at Beacon Hill or Old John Tower an ancient mountain landscape has been uncovered by millions of years of erosion. The old hard rocks which project through the thin soil cover on the hills of Charnwood were once covered by the thick sediments which have produced the fertile farmland at lower levels.

Leave the summit of the hill via a gap in the rock outcrops on the western side. The path skirts below a sizeable crag and soon joins a wide stony track which gradually descends past a conifer plantation. At lower levels the sandy soil supports birch woodland and on the final stretch leading to the lower car park rhododendrons have been introduced.

Leave the lower car park and turn right along the road to the T-junction at the B591. A shorter alternative to the full walk, which saves about one mile, can be taken here. Simply turn right on the B591 and continue on the Broombriggs Farm Trail beginning at the trail car park.

The longer route turns left to Woodhouse Eaves. At the Bull's Head, turn right down the main street of the village. It must be admitted that Woodhouse Eaves is a rather undistinguished sort of place. There are two public houses, a few shops, and at least two convalescent homes. The architectural gem of the village is the Baptist church. A chapel has stood on the site since the eighteenth century, but today there is a modern octagonal building with a lantern roof which is both simple and elegant.

Look out next for Maplewell Road on the right. At the corner is a line of neat stone Victorian almhouses which would have pleased Sir John Betjeman. Walk along this road and turn right up Mill Road. This climbs to a gate beyond which it is unsurfaced. It crosses Windmill Hill below the top, but the ultra-curious could make a detour through the oak trees to see the windmill. Be prepared for a disappointment, though, for all that is left is the stone base. A protrud-

Broombriggs Farm commands extensive views across the Leicestershire countryside

ing fang of Charnian rock nearby will yield some amusing scrambles, perhaps some consolation.

Descend to pick up the Broombriggs Farm Trail which will be seen coming up from the car park to a gate. It continues across a stile set in a stone wall alongside the continuation of Mill Lane. Cross the stile onto a headland path which descends to the next stile in the far boundary wall. The trail is easy to follow once the symbols on the waymark posts are understood. An attempt seems to have been made to separate pedestrians from horseriders; equestrian paths are marked with a horseshoe symbol and paths for walkers have a footprint.

Quite apart from the interest of its information boards the trail is worth following for its scenic attractions. The picnic site enjoys a fine open position looking out over Swithland Reservoir and Buddon Hill. The character of the immediate surroundings is of fertile farmland with some fine deciduous trees.

The farm trail reaches its highest point on Broombriggs Hill and then descends along the edge of a large field to a stile and then a wicket gate set in a stone wall. Another short descent ends at the farm drive which soon joins the B591. Users of the trail car park will find a path leading through the wood directly to it.

To return to Beacon Hill go through the gate on the north side of the B591 opposite the farm drive. Once through the gate turn left along a sandy path which is wide and clear. It keeps close to the road for some distance, passing through thin birch woodland. Eventually the birches give way to bracken and open grassland as the path gains height.

The small crags around the summit of Beacon Hill come into view. The hill once had an Iron Age fort and some sections of bank are discernible on this approach. A shelter belt of trees on the left marks the position of the upper car park and it is possible to avoid ascending the hill a second time by making directly for them.

Walk 16
BRADGATE HOUSE
LEICESTERSHIRE
7 miles

Bradgate House was a brick-built Tudor mansion begun about 1490. The brick construction was new at that time. The bricks were made from local Keuper Marl and there are still traces of the old clay pit at the southern end of Cropston Reservoir. Today the house is a ruin, but sufficient remains to give an idea of its former grandeur.

The most famous person associated with Bradgate was Lady Jane Grey. The octagonal tower near the chapel is known as Lady Jane's Tower and was probably her private retreat.

Bradgate is now a country park and the public enjoys free access for recreational purposes to an area of ancient parkland over which a herd of 300 deer roam and which has many natural features of great beauty and interest.

The walk begins from the Old John car park four miles south of Loughborough, near Newtown Linford. The entrance to the car park lies on the Newtown Linford to Woodhouse Eaves road. Start by going through the wicket gate in the wall and climb the hill to Old John Tower. This is the highest place on the walk and a superb vantage point. A toposcope near the tower gives details of surrounding landmarks.

This site originally had a windmill, recorded on a map of 1754, with the name Old John. Tradition tells of celebrations at the coming of age of the Earl of Stamford's eldest son. A large bonfire was built around a pole topped by a tar barrel.

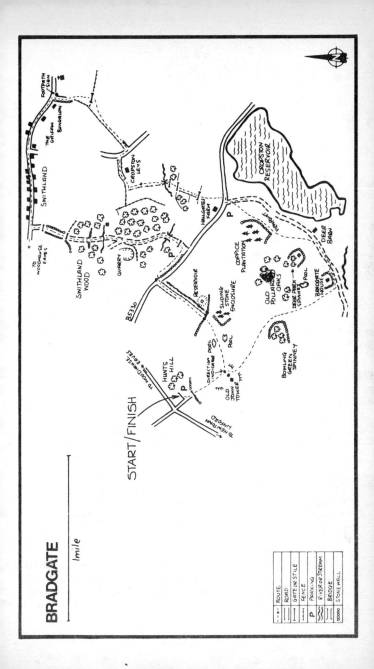

The pole toppled onto the head of an ageing miller named Old John, fatally injuring him. The present tower is his memorial.

Many paths radiate from the tower; take the one heading roughly north-east which passes near a dewpond. It continues alongside a plantation to a wicket gate set in a stone wall.

From here the path follows a green lane bordered with birches and oaks, leading to the B5330. Cross the road and enter Swithland Wood through a squeezer stile in the stone wall. Immediately turn right, cross a plank bridge and over Swithland Wood car park.

Opposite the car park entrance, take the gate which leads to a bridleway going into the wood. The bridleway crosses a stream and climbs gradually through woodland which here is chiefly oak, a rare survivor from the medieval forest which once covered most of central England.

The fence which shortly appears on the left of the track guards the edge of an old slate quarry. Swithland slate, an attractive grey-green, can be seen on the roofs of the older houses in Swithland village.

A plaque set in a stone to the right of the bridleway records that the wood was secured as a National Heritage in 1931 by the Rotary Club of Leicester. After passing the plaque, take the right-hand path where it divides. The new path crosses a stream and goes through an old wall to a stile in a fence at the edge of the wood. From here a short stretch of lane leads to the road on the outskirts of Swithland village. The village straddles the road for nearly a mile; its church lies beyond its eastern end.

Turn right at the road. There are some fine old houses to be admired as you follow the village street, and near the end on the left stands a circular tower – possibly a toll house, yet that seems unlikely. Beyond the tower is the Griffin Inn, and soon a signposted footpath leads south alongside the garden of a bungalow. It passes through two wicket gates and enters a field – keep near the right-hand edge when crossing to the white wicket gate. Half a mile away to the east is Swithland

Bradgate House, now a ruin, was once the home of Lady Jane Grey

Hall, and in the park visible in front of it is a solitary stump known as the Lantern Cross.

The path now goes through the white wicket gate and keeps to the headland along the right-hand fence. You reach a surfaced road almost opposite the drive of Cropston Leys. Continue on the drive passing the entrance of the house which is screened by a tall conifer hedge. The path continues along the side of a field and eventually enters Swithland Wood, but 150 yards short of the wood our walk diverts along another path, the course of which is clearly marked by a line of trees, surely once part of a continuous hedge.

The path crosses a stream, enters a spinney, then goes through a wicket gate and a stile. The path is awkwardly constrained between a barbed wire fence and a tall hedge, but the next stile leads to easier going between two wire fences, and Hallgates Farm, standing beside the B5330, comes into sight. Barring the way to the farm is a maze of wooden rail fences which would pose an awkward route-finding problem but for numerous waymark arrows and stiles. Follow these to the road near the entrance of Hallgates car park.

The walk now enters Bradgate Park. A tarmac road leads tamely alongside Cropston Reservoir, and the better alternative is a grassy path going uphill and passing close to Coppice Plantation. The extra effort it demands is amply repaid by the view from a craggy outcrop at the southern end of the coppice. Over to the west here are some ancient pollarded oaks. Pollarding of oaks was carried out to provide firewood, but tradition has it that these trees were beheaded by estate woodmen as a sign of mourning after the execution of Lady Jane Grey.

Descend from the viewpoint to the road near the Deer Barn and follow it to Bradgate House ruins. The path up to Old John follows the western facade of the ruins, climbing gradually and passing to the east of a walled spinney. The tower comes into view and the way back to the car park will be familiar from the start of the walk.

Walk 17
HARLESTONE
NORTHAMPTONSHIRE
6½ miles

Harlestone is the collective name for a cluster of settlements which lie west of the A428 Rugby to Northampton road. The first house builders here were fortunate in having Duston stone at hand. It weathers into a pale buff and sometimes ochre colour and it can be seen at its best in the walls of the thirteenth-century village church. Most of the old cottages are thatched and the combination of these traditional materials is chiefly what gives the village its charm. Harlestone House was demolished in 1940 but the influence of its owner is still present in the way the parkland has been preserved as open space between the different parts of the village.

At the village's western end is a perfect fifteenth-century dovecote. Dovecotes provided fresh meat for the table during the winter months to relieve the monotonous diet of smoked and salted meat. This one is built in two stages separated by a projecting string course which deterred vermin.

The walk begins at Harlestone Heath two and a half miles north of Northampton along the A428. A layby opposite the entrance to the woods can be used for parking cars.

Although the woodlands are privately owned, several public rights of way pass through. One leads from the gate at the roadside through the wood along a wide ride which eventually turns sharp left and continues to a sawmill. Leave the ride at this bend and go straight ahead on a wide unsurfaced track across Dallington Heath. The character of the woodland changes; a line of mature beech trees graces the left-

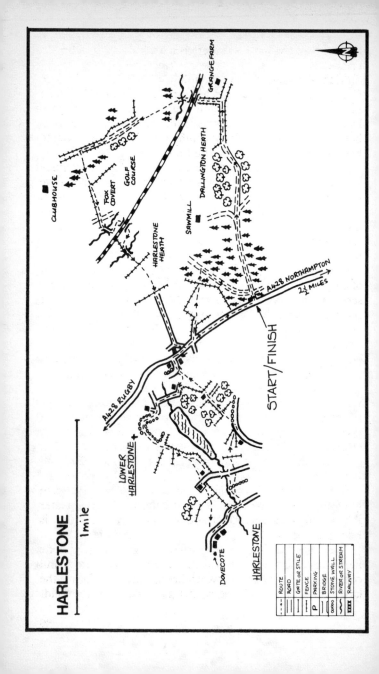

HARLESTONE

1 mile

CLUBHOUSE

GOLF COURSE

FOX COVERT

GRANGE FARM

DALLINGTON HEATH

SAWMILL

HARLESTONE HEATH

A428 NORTHAMPTON
2½ MILES

START/FINISH

A428 RUGBY

LOWER HARLESTONE

DOVECOTE

HARLESTONE

	ROUTE
	ROAD
	GATE OR STILE
	FENCE
P	PARKING
	BRIDGE
	STONE WALL
	RIVER OR STREAM
	RAILWAY

hand side of the path and there is a scattering of birches on the heath.

At the edge of the woodland follow a fenced grassy track to Grange Farm. Here a sharp left turn leads downhill under a railway bridge and onto a golf course where the clear path leading across is a right of way. It crosses a stream and goes between two small stands of conifers. From here it is well to keep a wary eye open for errant golf balls.

The path runs uphill to the relative safety of an oak spinney and continues along an unsurfaced lane. Two footpaths leave the lane to cross the golf course again. Ignore the first, starting at the northern end of the spinney. The walk takes the next path 300 yards further along the lane. The exact spot is marked by a stile on the left which is opposite a field gate on the right.

Cross the stile and walk over the golf course to a shelter belt of conifers and continue straight ahead to a patch of tangled scrub at the edge of Fox Covert. Find a way through the scrub to a wicket gate which leads into the wood; go through, and follow a clearly defined path on the edge of the wood. Continue straight ahead where a ride comes in on the left. The woodland path ends by crossing a bridge over a stream; skirt the field to arrive at a bridge under a railway.

Gates bar the way on either side of the railway bridge; the second one is waymarked. Follow the direction of the arrow across a small field to a footbridge and another waymarked gate. From here the path is waymarked at every gate. It crosses two fields and then follows a fenced lane. At the last gate in the lane turn left to meet the A428 near the Fox and Hounds.

The Fox and Hounds is a well-proportioned Georgian building and very inviting. We shall return to this point later in the walk. The village straddling the main road here is known as Lower Harlestone.

Leave the main road at the turning opposite the telephone kiosk. A narrow lane starts alongside a thatched cottage and continues to a sharp bend which has a cattle grid. Leave the lane here, go through the wicket gate and cross the field.

This charming 15th Century dovecote stands on the western edge of Harlestone Village.

Fork right down a sunken way to a ford. From here the narrow lane winds round to a group of picturesque houses grouped around the village school.

Continue now on the walled footpath which leads past the church and enters the park. The footpaths across the park have been surfaced and one is spoiled for choice. Keep near the wall of the former stable block on a path leading to a wicket gate. The path is confined between fences for a short distance and then it divides. Take the right-hand path which leads to the village hall. Continue through the wicket gates across the next field. Here again there is a choice; try the path which strikes out diagonally due west across the field. It ends at a gate on the lane 100 yards or so from the fifteenth-century dovecote.

From the dovecote, retrace your steps to the field gate and continue along the lane to a bridge over the stream. Beyond, take the wicket gate in the wall, cross a small field to another wicket set in a stone wall, and continue to the next lane. Across the lane is a wicket placed alongside a cottage drive. Go through and cross the field to a stile and on to a second stile near a row of houses on the lane.

A few yards to the left of the stile there is a field gate set in a wall. Go through and cross the field to a wicket gate set in a wooden fence. A wide straight path now leads through a wood to a cottage. Cross the grass verge in front of the cottage and go through the field gate. The path follows the line of a wooden fence at first and then joins the outward route near the wicket at the lane leading from Lower Harlestone.

Retrace the outward route to the Fox and Hounds.

The A428 has a footpath along its entire length to the layby at the start of the walk. A quieter way of getting back to your car begins near the side road to Brington. A short stretch of unsurfaced lane leads to a field gate. From here a path crosses the field to a wicket gate on the edge of the woodland of Harlestone Heath. Go through into the woodland and turn right along the first major ride. This gives a pleasant level route to the entrance gate of the woods where the walk began.

Walk 18
ASHBY ST LEDGERS
WARWICKSHIRE
7 miles

The most picturesque parts of the village of Ashby St Ledgers are the church and manor house. The exterior of the church is chiefly fourteenth century. Inside are a Jacobean pulpit and pews, and a complete cycle of faded wall paintings of the Passion dating from around 1500.

On the north side of the church is a Tudor period stone gatehouse, with a timber-framed upper storey, which once guarded the entrance to the manor house. The present entrance is through the courtyard gates facing onto the road. The house's style is Elizabethan or Jacobean yet only the centre section is original. The left wing was designed by Sir Edwin Lutyens who was also responsible for the design of other buildings in the village dating from around 1909–10. Walk round the bend in the road to catch a glimpse of the beautiful gardens and the seventeenth-century 'Ipswich House'. Built in Ipswich, this was re-erected here by the second Lord Wimbourne.

The starting point is the village of Braunston, east of the A45(T), three miles north-west of Daventry. At the eastern end of the village, parking space can be found on service roads or on the wide grass verges of the land leading eastwards out of the village.

Start at the triangular island near the old village school, now the village hall. Leave the village along Ashby Road where the houses end at a playground. The road continues in the same direction between hedgerows, finally losing its

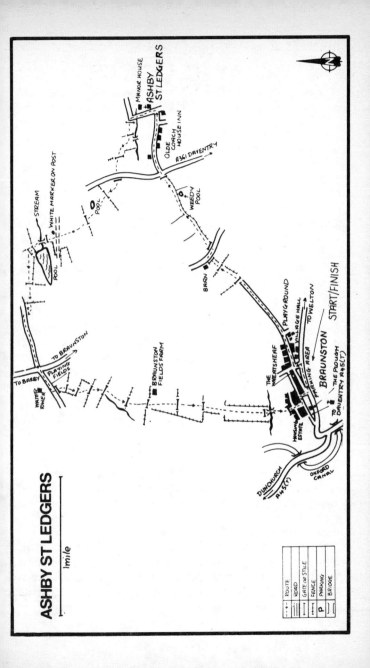

ASHBY ST LEDGERS

1 mile

MANOR HOUSE
ASHBY ST LEDGERS
OLDE COACH HOUSE INN
A361 DAVENTRY
WEED¥ POOL
POOL
WHITE MARKER ON POST
STREAM
POOL
BARN
PLAYGROUND
VILLAGE HALL
TOWELTON
START/FINISH
BRAUNSTON
THE WHEATSHEAF
PARKING AREA
TO THE PLOUGH
DAVENTRY A45(T)
BRAUNSTON FIELDS FARM
TO BRAUNSTON
PLAYING FIELDS
TO BARBY
WATER TOWER
DUNCHURCH A45(T)
OXFORD CANAL

	ROUTE
	ROAD
	GATE OR STILE
	FENCE
P	PARKING
	BRIDGE

metalled surface. At the lane end is a metal wicket gate, then the path crosses two fields, via wicket gates set in the hedgerows, to a surfaced lane.

Turn right for a few yards to another wicket on the left and continue along a headland bridleway to the crest of a slight rise. The hedgerow on the line of the path and the one coming in on the left contain the stumps of elm trees, a sad reminder of fine old trees that fell victim to Dutch Elm Disease.

At the top of the rise the view ahead is quite extensive. Ashby St Ledgers can be seen, with the Watford Gap beyond. The bridleway follows the hedge downhill, passing a small pool, ending on the edge of a spinney at the side of the A361. There is a wicket gate at the roadside and directly opposite is the lane leading into Ashby St Ledgers.

Just beyond The Coach House Inn, on the opposite side of the street, are thatched cottages designed by Edwin Lutyens – an attractive prelude to the major architectural attractions of the village.

Continue to the church and manor house, and on to a field gate where the road turns sharply right around the manor grounds. Go through the gate and follow the stream to the left to a stile in the hedge. Over the hedge another footpath from the village comes across the stream by a footbridge.

Turn away from the footbridge and set off diagonally across the field to a stile and plank bridge. Cross the next field to a signposted stile on the A361. Opposite, a signpost marks the start of a path leading to Barby. Follow the signpost direction first through a gate and then to the next stile with a plank bridge set in a hedgerow.

The next section of the route is probably the most awkward for route-finding. There are waymarks but you need acute vision to actually spot them. First cross the next field and keep in single file if it carries a crop. Aim to the left of a tree-fringed pool and a waymarked stile will appear.

The path now crosses parkland with fine old deciduous trees. One of these, in the far distance, carries a white waymark. Take heart and set off in the hope that it will soon be in view. After the waymarked tree cross an estate track

In Ashby St Ledgers, weathered limestone and half-timbering have combined to produce attractive buildings

and find a marker on a tubular metal post. From here aim for the gate at the edge of the wood. Go through the gate, cross the stream and leave the wood via two more field gates.

Direction finding now becomes straightforward; turn left and keep near the edge of the wood to the next field. Go through the gate into it, cross the stile visible in the opposite hedge then walk diagonally right to a last stile at the lane.

The path continues across the lane to Barby, but this walk keeps on the lane to a cross-roads. Go straight across, keeping the playing field on the left, to where a signpost on the left points to the footpath leading to Braunston. There should be no difficulty in following this path across a series of stiles in the hedgerows of the first three small fields.

The fourth field drops away into a hollow. In the bottom of the hollow a gate marks the continuation of the path. Keep near the right-hand hedge, where a brook has appeared, to the next stile. Braunston Fields Farm is now in view. There are two field gates in the hedge near it; aim for the gate nearest the farm.

Cross the next field beyond Braunston Fields Farm and now the spire of Braunston Church makes a perfect homing point. Aim directly towards it and you should be on line to encounter gates and stiles which allow access to each successive field. The lower end of the last field in the succession is fringed by a line of pollarded willows, indicators of the line of a stream which has to be crossed. The stile and footbridge are in the lower left corner of the field.

One more field remains to be crossed to a stile at the edge of a housing estate. The path from it runs between back gardens into Countryside which in turn leads to Ash Way, a cul-de-sac, but walkers may escape from it via a footpath with metal barriers. The footpath arrives in a street which runs parallel with the main village thoroughfare. Turn left, take the first right to emerge in the main street near the parking area marked on the map.